Zentangle Art Story II Coloring Book
Floral Series II

Created by Anna Zubarev

Anna Zubarev

Copyright ©2020 Anna Zubarev

All rights reserved.

ISBN: 9798554928635

A FLORAL COLLECTION OF HAND-DRAWN

ZENTANGLE INSPIRED ILLUSTRATIONS

FOR COLORING.

ABOUT THE CREATOR

A Brooklyn, NY - based Illustrator whose focus to create with ink fine-liner pens to illustrate the love and passion she has for the Zentangle Inspired world.

From a hobby, this became a full-time passion. Every single illustration created is a hand-drawn illustration and no stock art or clip art was used in creating these motifs.

This book was created to let other people inspire to color and have a glimpse of the joy Anna experiences while creating these illustrations, so it means the world to her that you've made this purchase.

Ignite your imagination and step into this magical floral imaginary world, where you can color beautifully thought out designs by using your choice of colored pencils, watercolors, gel pens or markers.

Enjoy it for years to come as each design is perforated and single- paged for you to hang up in your home, office or give as a present.

The joy and inspiration you will experience are extremely important to Anna so she invites you to leave your feedback and connect with her on social media.

Anna's biggest beliefs are with love, patience and passion anything is possible!

New Updates are posted daily on her social channels, where you can see how all these drawings become alive.

Come and see it for your self in the videos, that Anna shares:

Instagram: Instagram.com/ZentangleArtStory

Facebook: Facebook.com/ZentangleArtStory

INTRODUCTON

In life, the journey of self-discovery everyone goes through. For me, throughout the years, I have dabbled in many areas, and while I learned a lot, I found myself unhappy. It wasn't until I discovered the world of Zentangle, where I felt my fulfillment. It was at that moment when I felt the need to inspire others to be happy doing what they love and what would make them happy.

My journey began one faithful day when a friend asked me to create a drawing. Throughout the years, I never had the time to fully invest my time in art, but this time, it felt different, and I believe my friend sparked my creativity to wake up.

This time in my life it was different, I was able to fill my days learning and practicing to master my skills, as I still do and practice daily drawings. I went all in this process of creation. It took a lot of time and a lot of patience to practice these skills that I can create today. Finding joy within every stroke, line, and fulfilling my desires to the fullest.

I had to share this joy I was experiencing with others.

With each piece of art, I create I leave apart of me in it. Music in my ears and the hush, at my home, I poured my heart and soul onto that blank canvas! The beautifully composed melody dancing in my ears and invading my space activated within me a love and passion I left somewhere in my happy childhood, and now I got to experienced the same joy once more. It was in that place of no judgment, clear mind I discovered a new me.

The beautiful thing about it is I also found that I could make a difference. The difference that brings others happiness as much as it does to me. To change one piece of the world one drawing at a time and leave my mark.

Enjoy this carefully crafted, hand-drawn designs that will bring you peace and healing for hours. Use colored pencils or markers and explore the possibilities. Get a glimpse into that part of my life when I draw and what makes me happy when I do it.

Feel the magic that will unfold right in front of your eyes when you begin coloring these illustrations. The same magic I am experiencing when I create these drawings and get to see the final results when I complete them.

The moment when your vision becomes your reality, and the final result of your vision, give you that satisfaction to the extent of childish excitement. Within these lines, you will find clarity, healing, peace, and happiness that I found. I hope to bring you even just a fraction of the joy that I feel when creating this art.

Within these pages, let inspiration take you to a new world, the world of Zentangle Art Story. Zentangle.

This book belongs to

_____

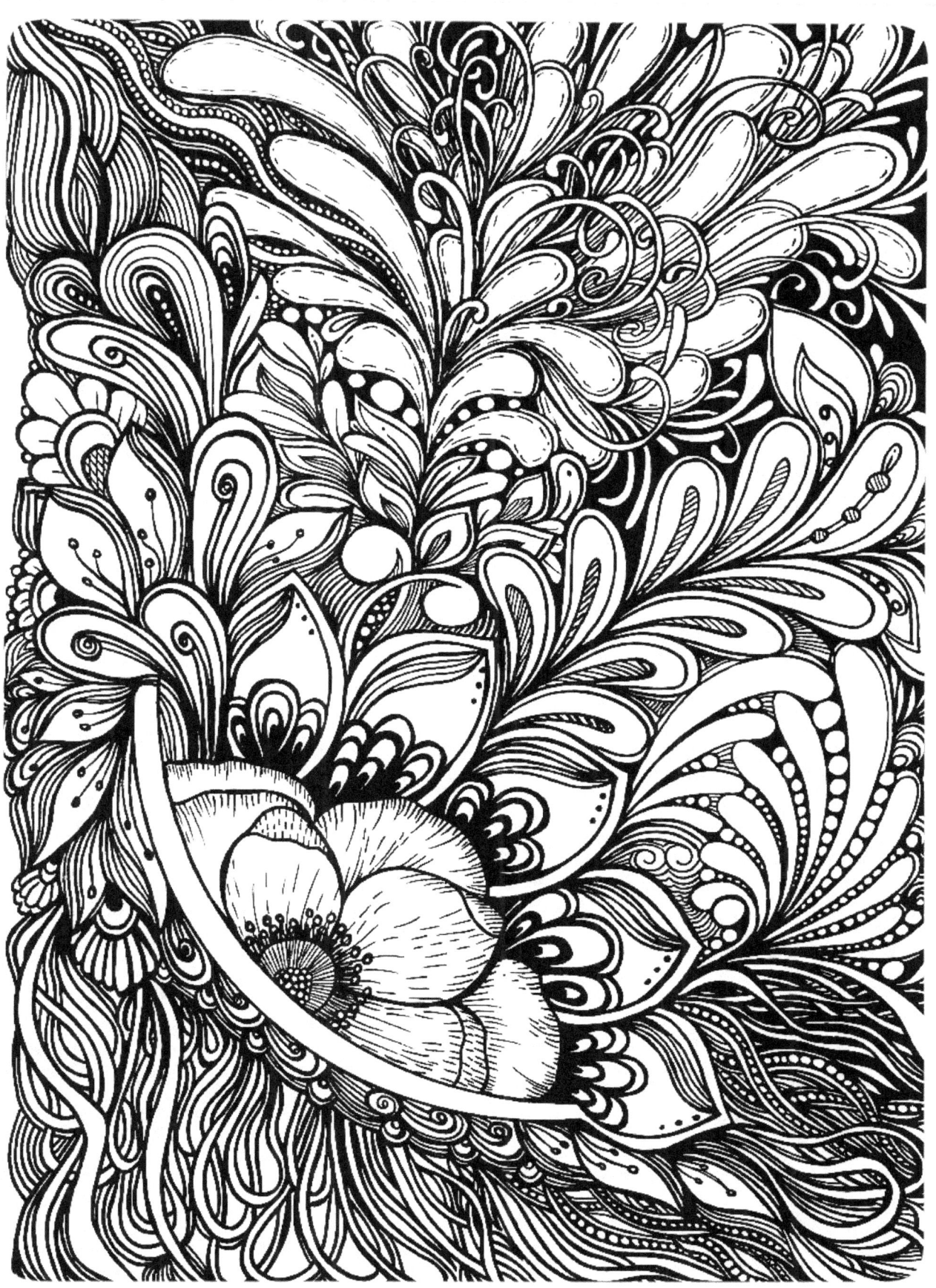

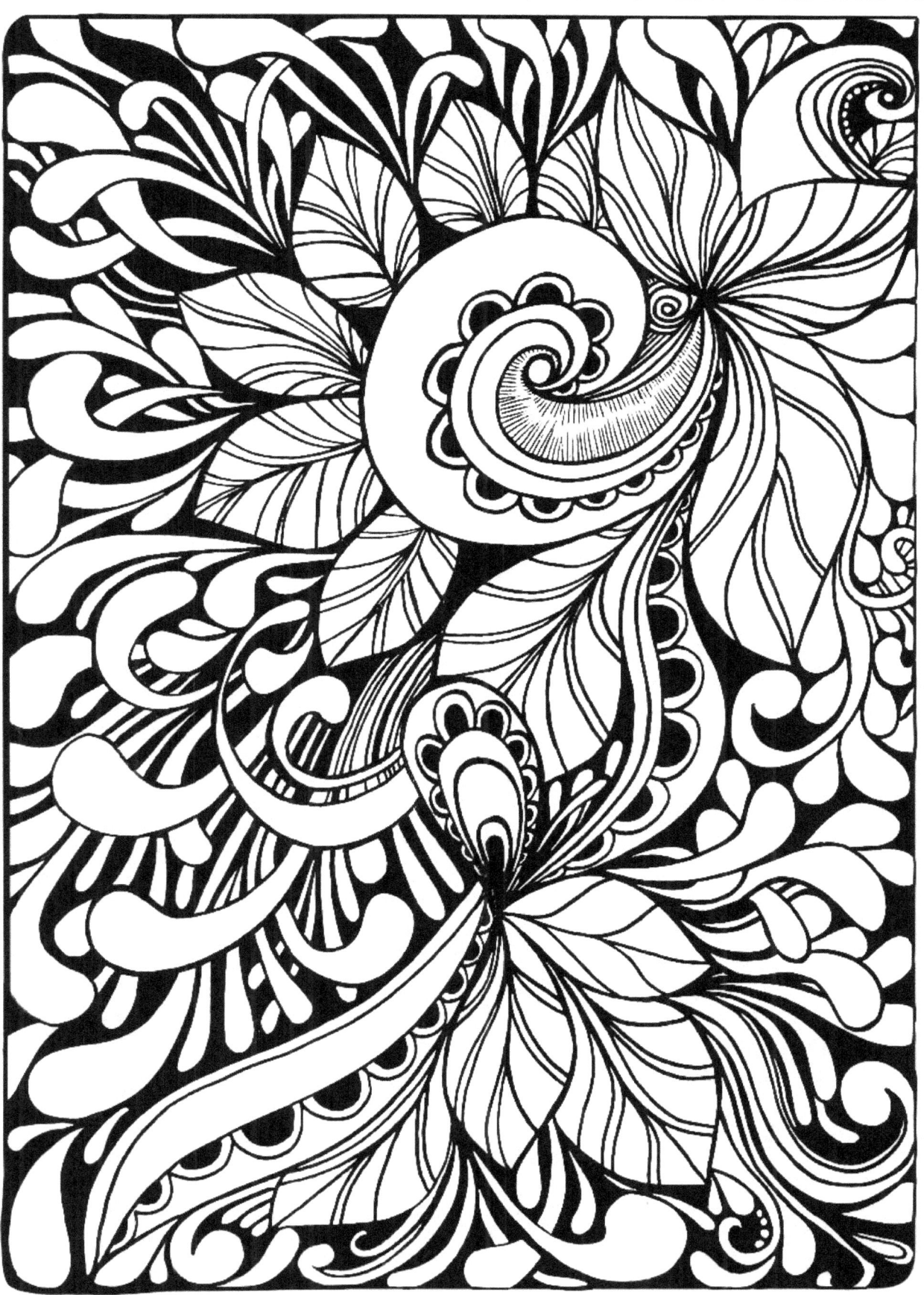

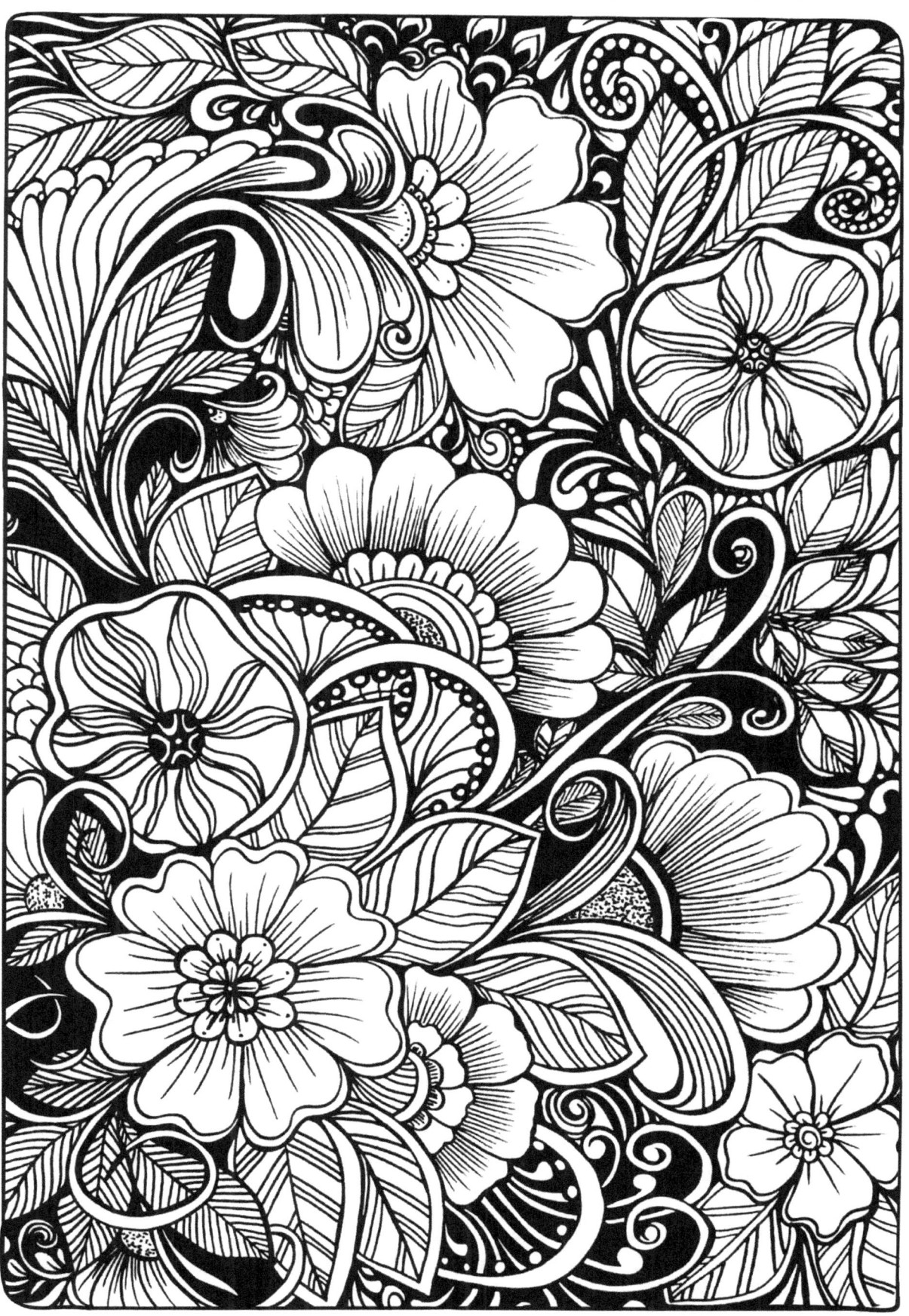

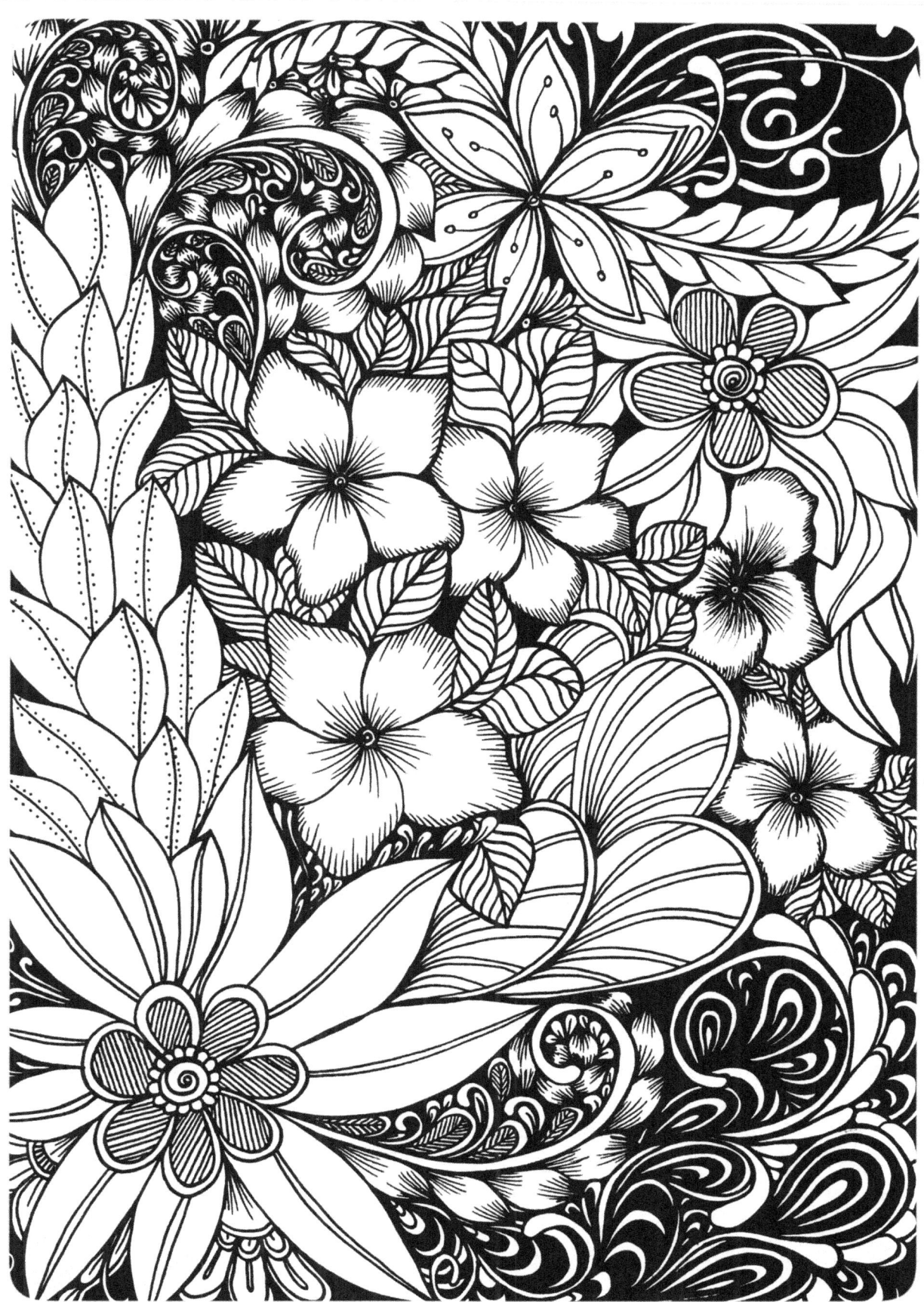

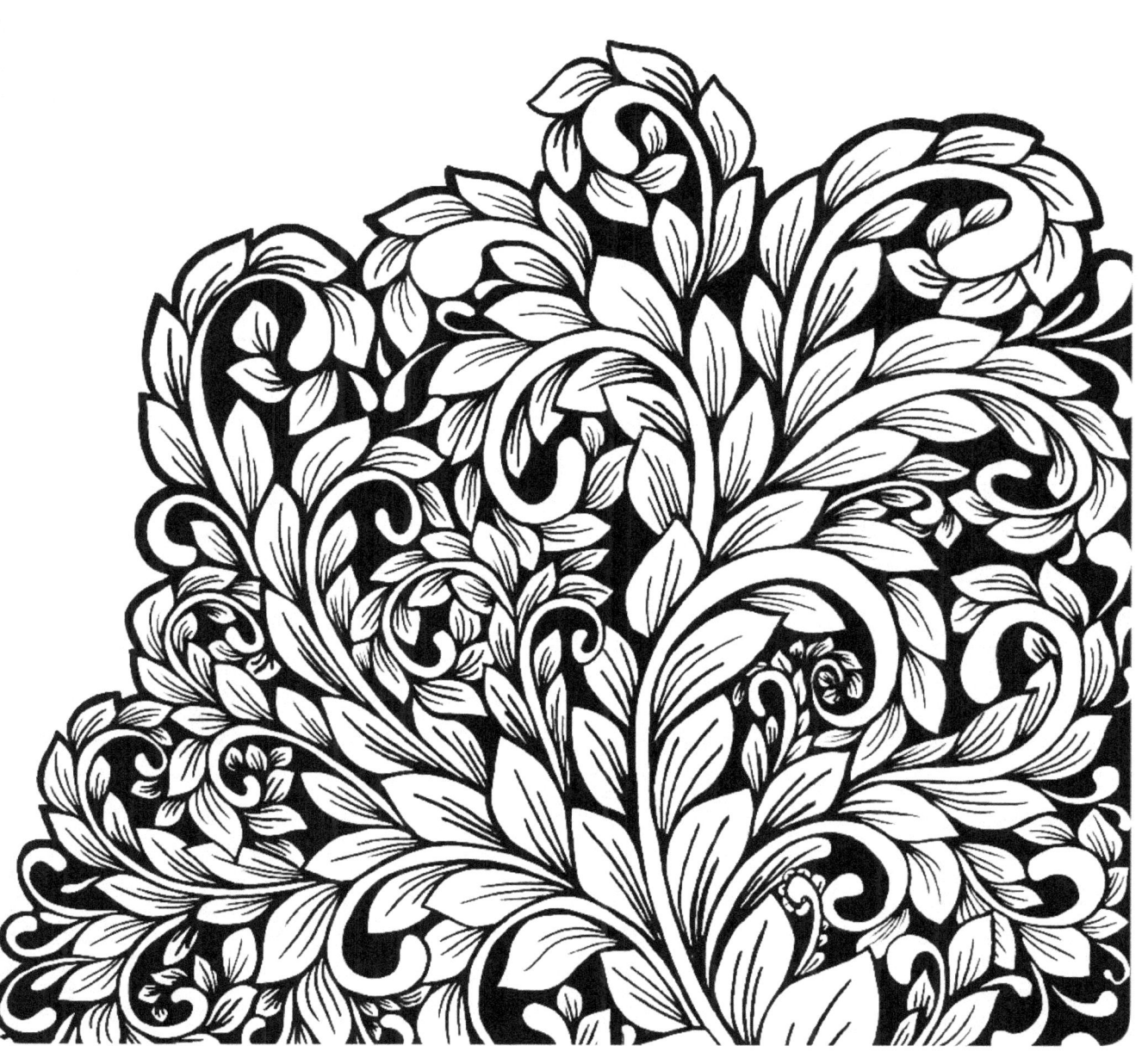

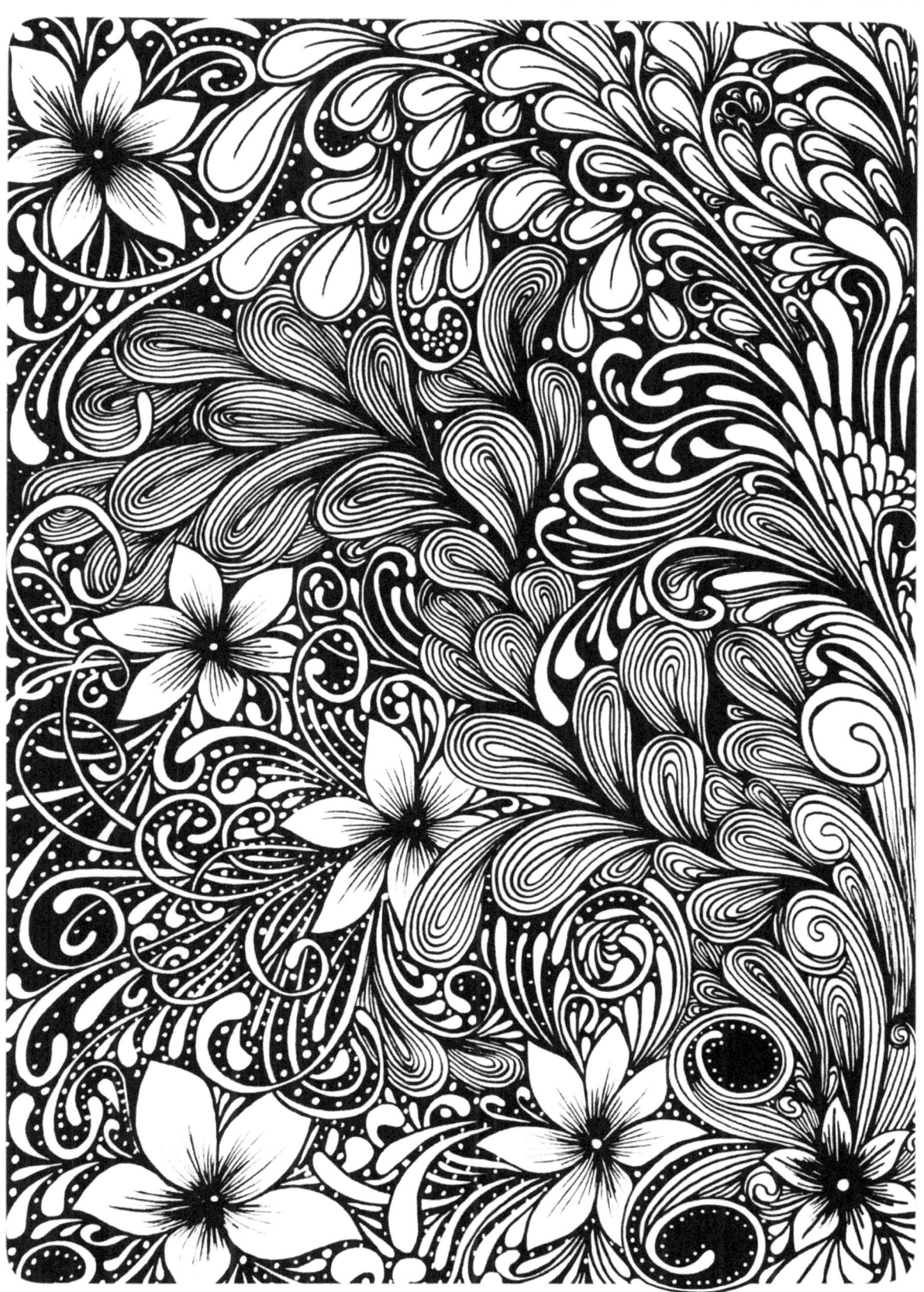

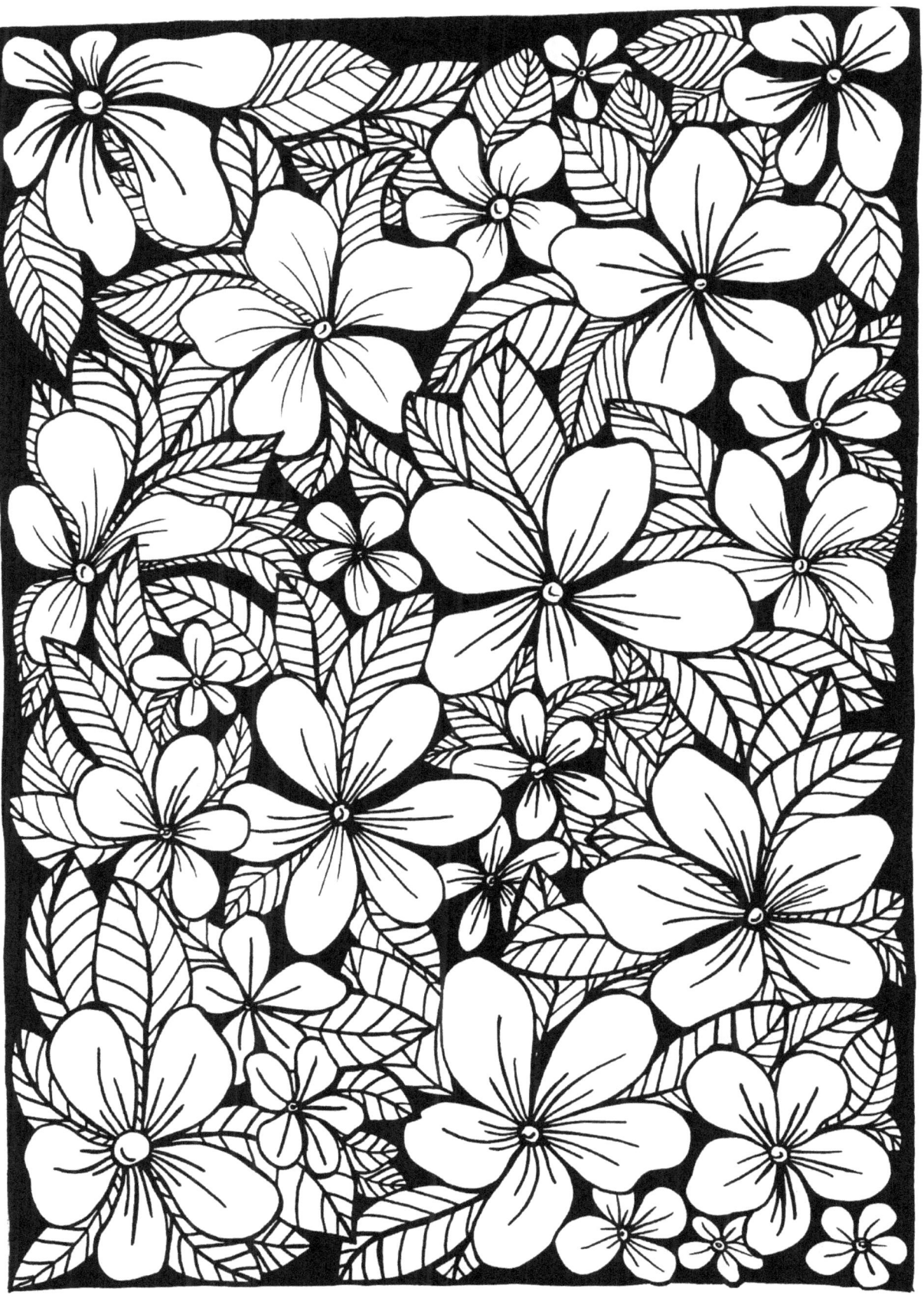

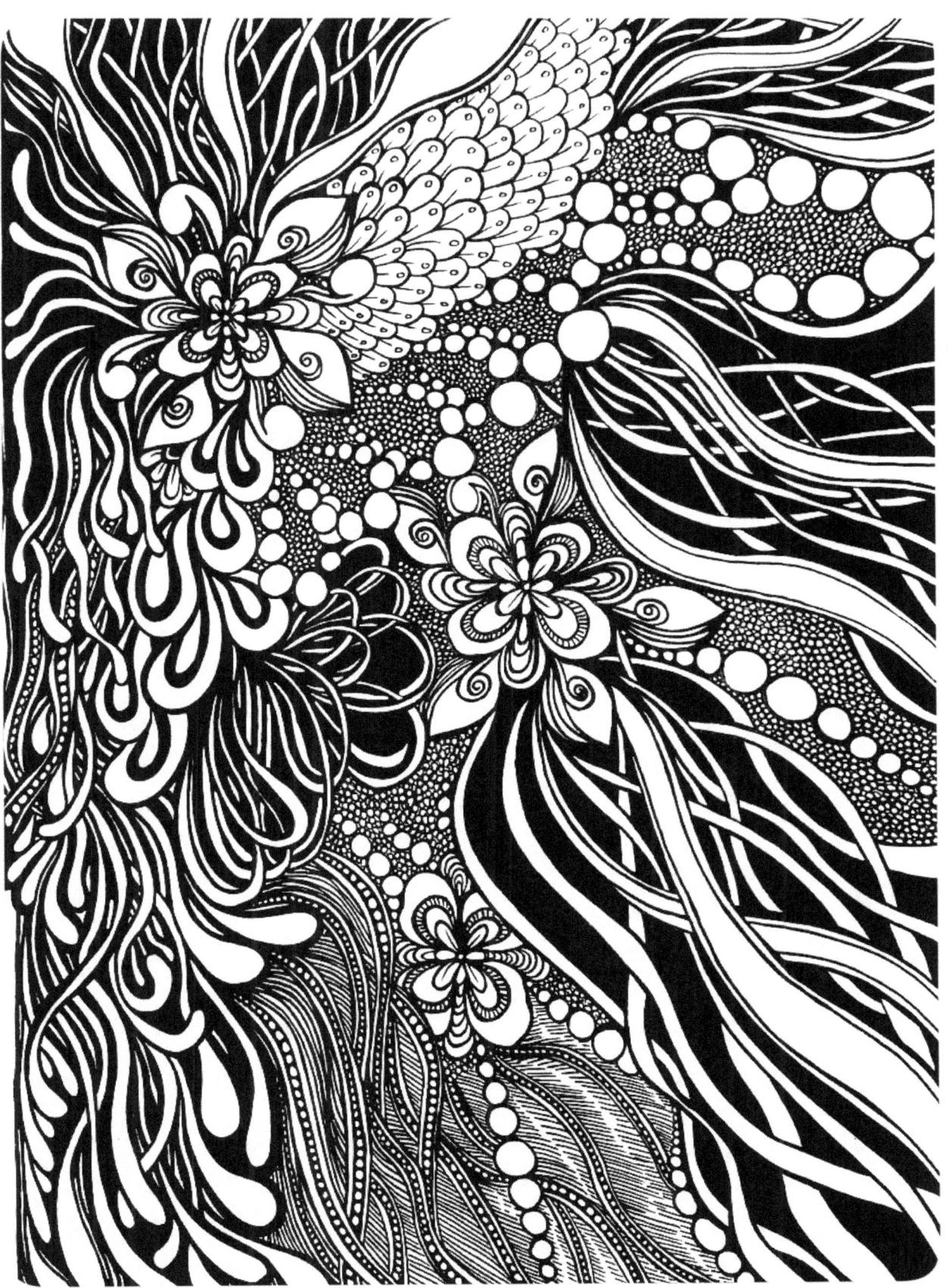

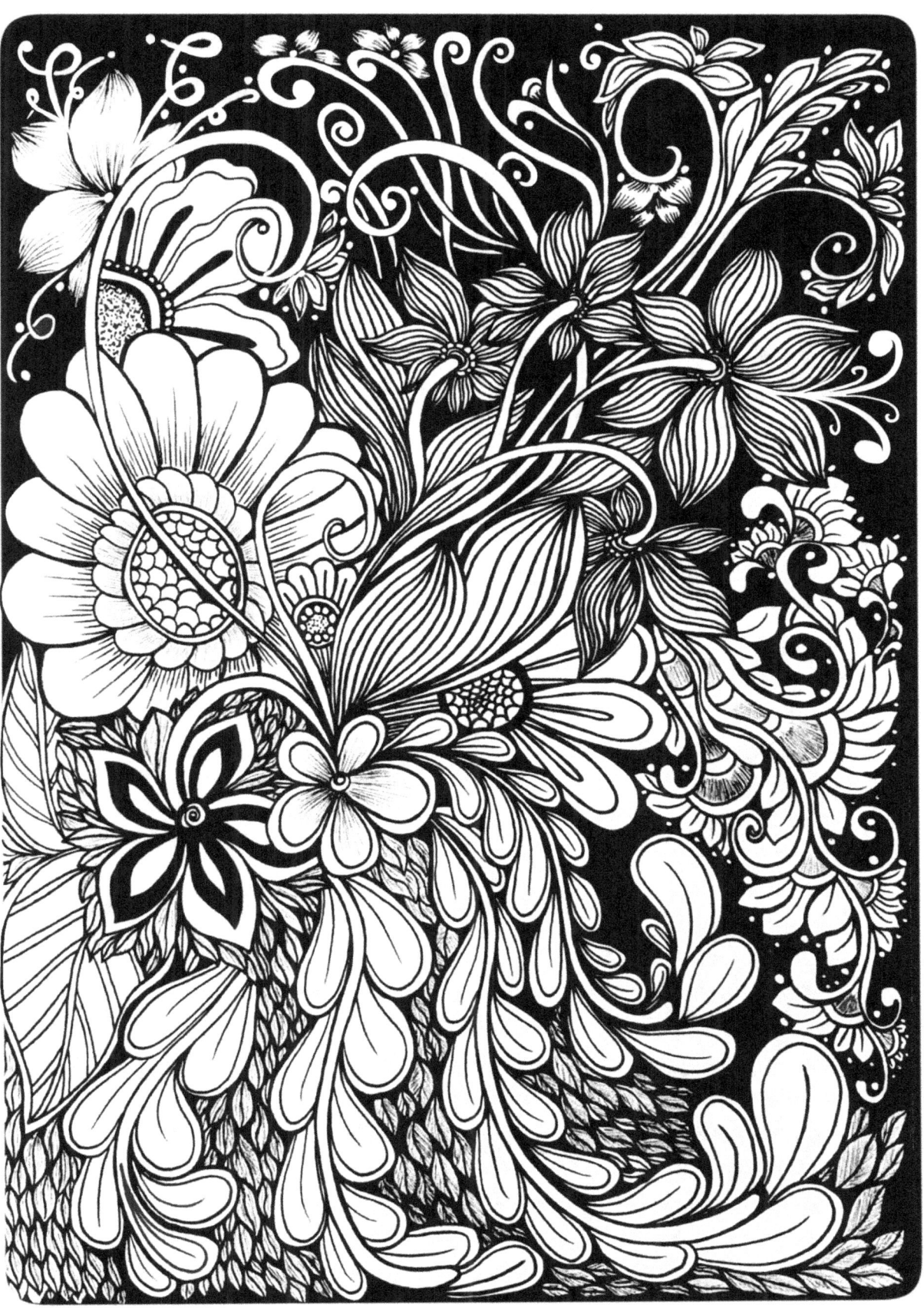

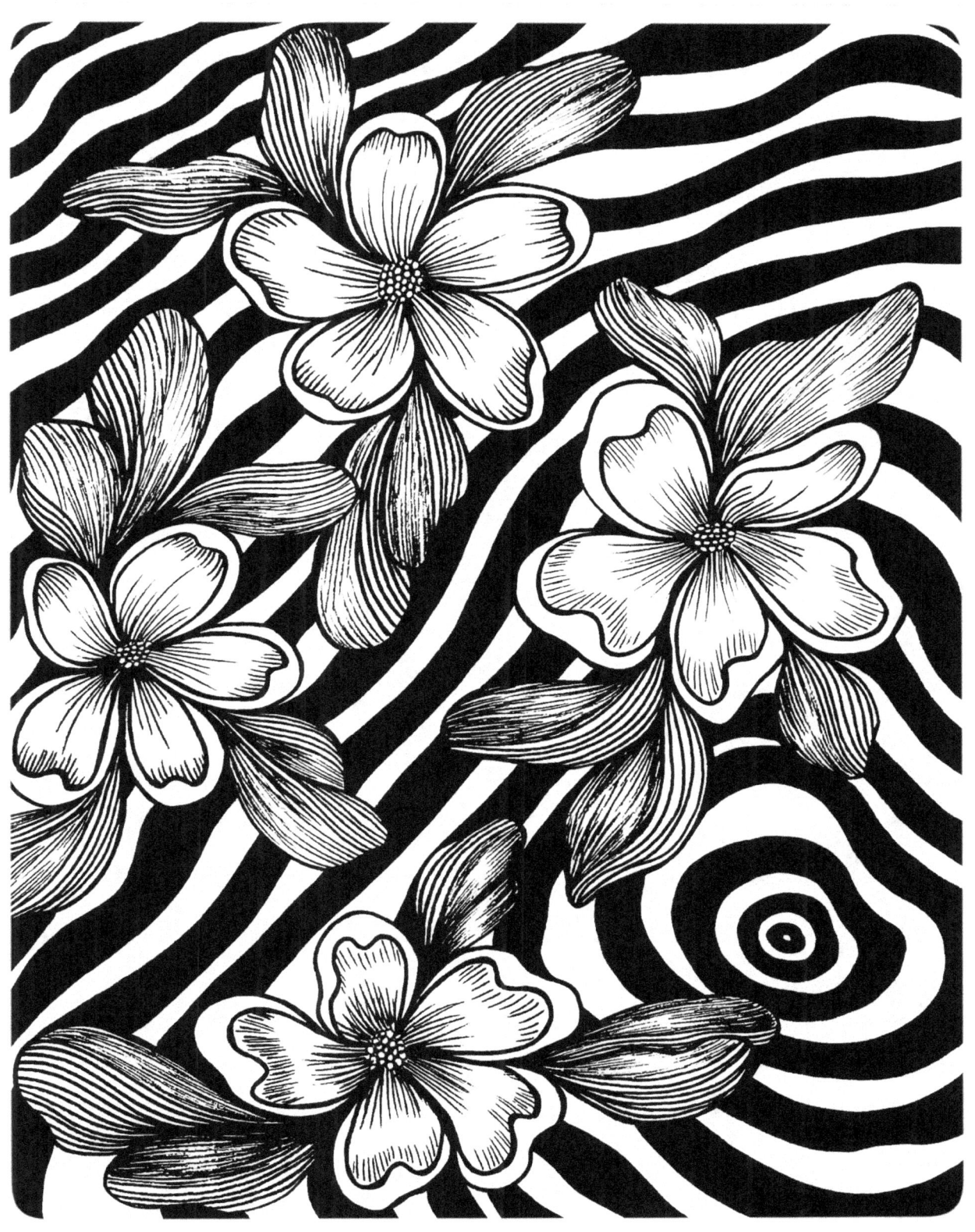

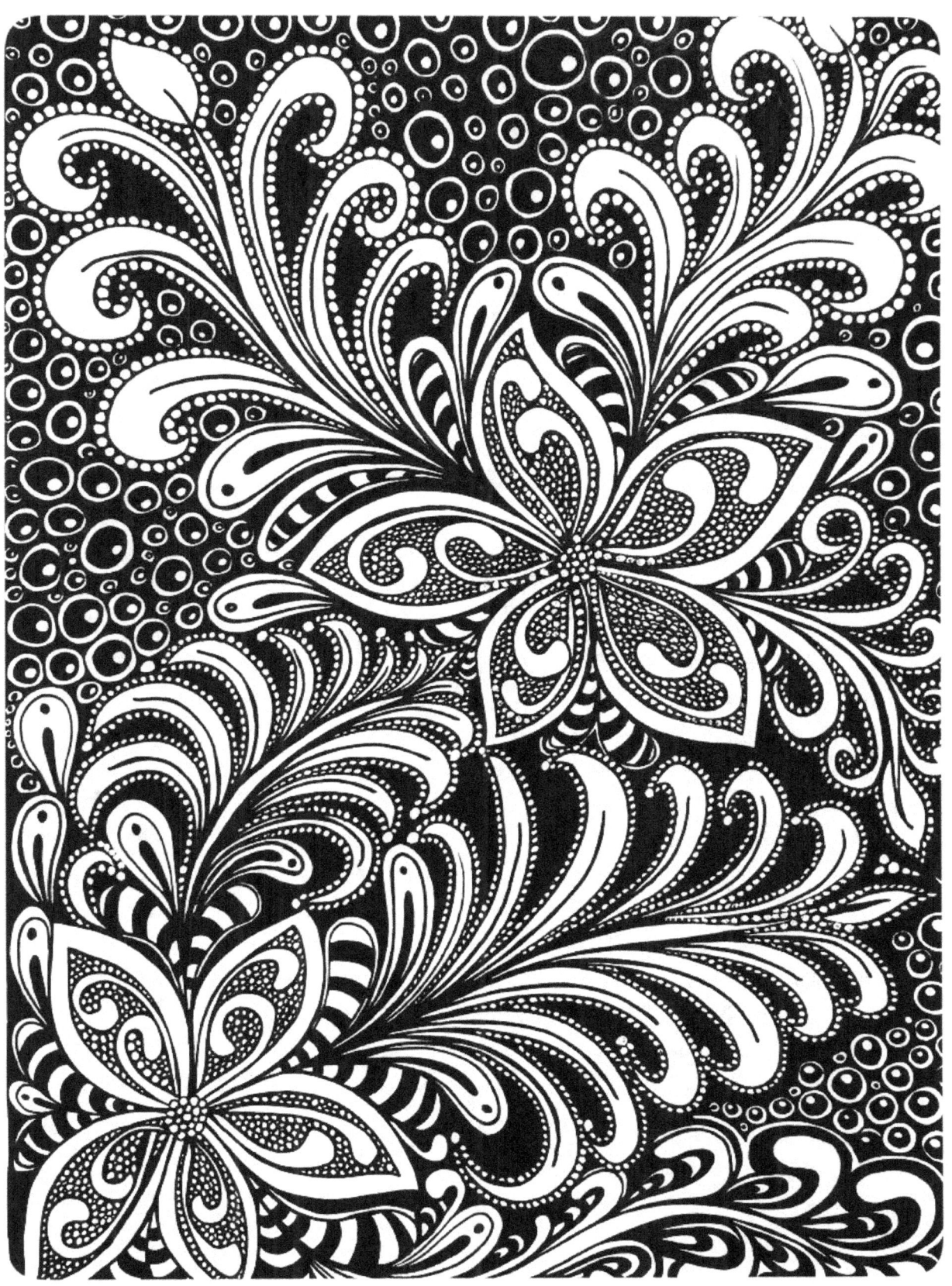

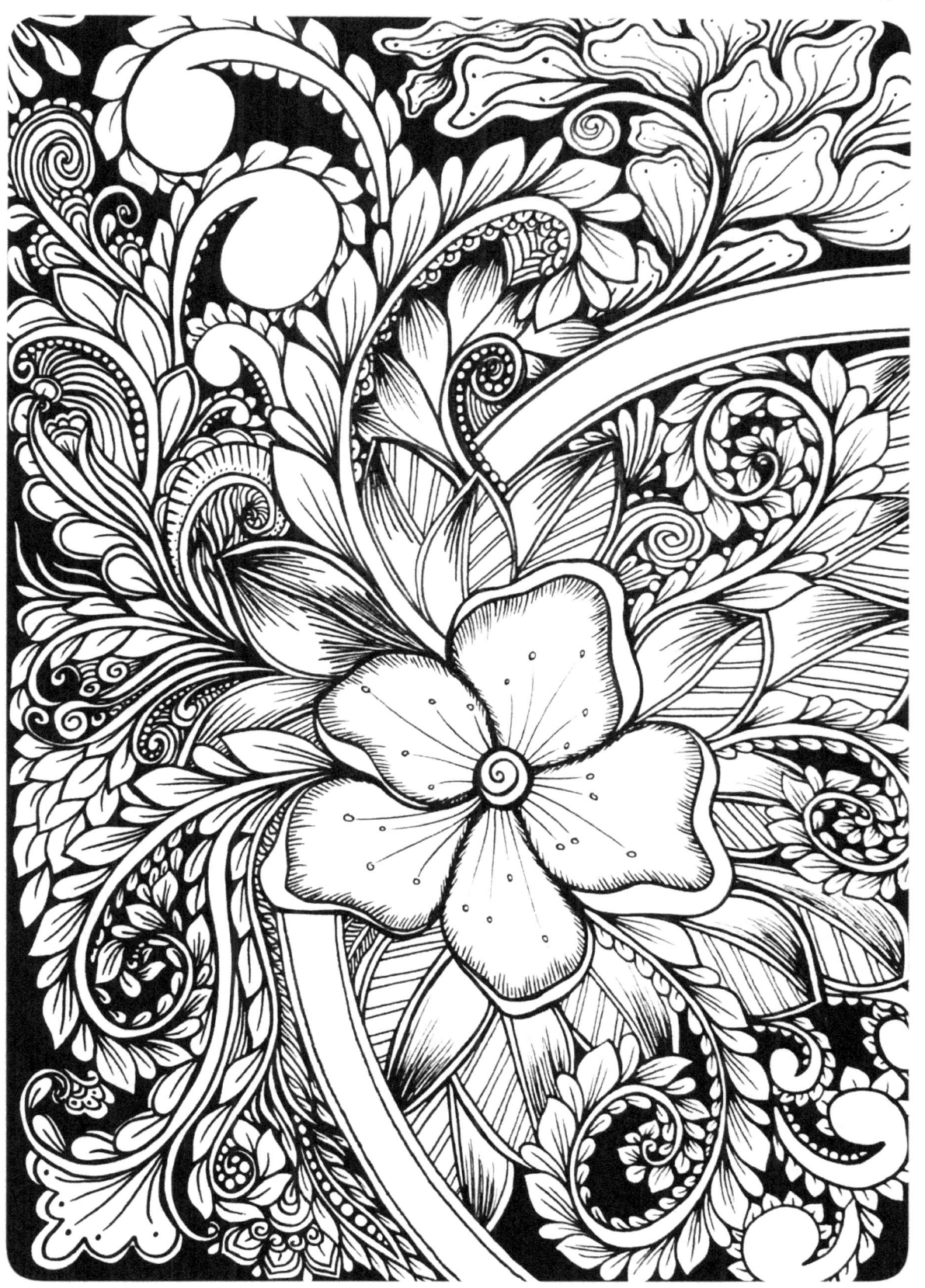

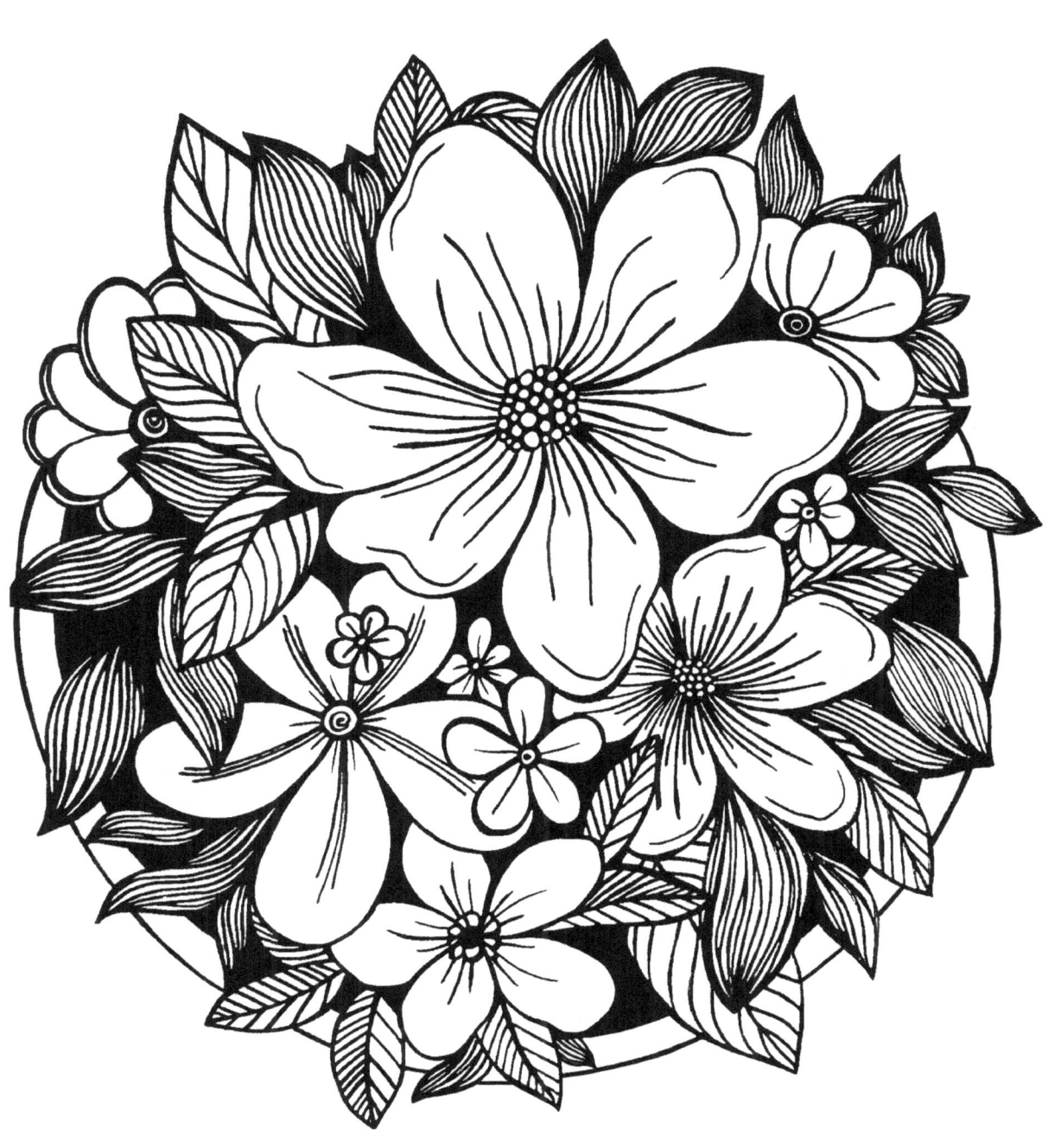

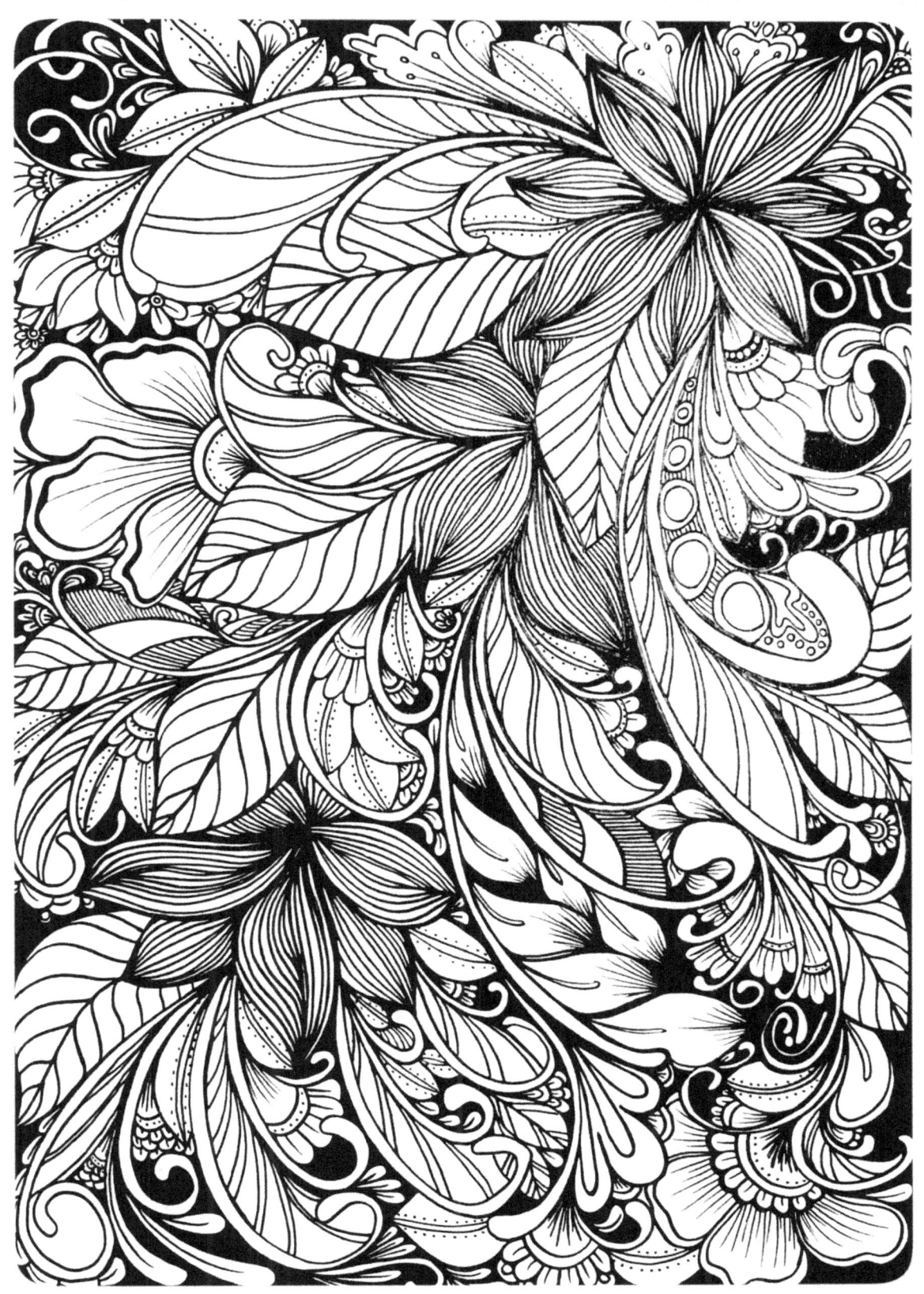

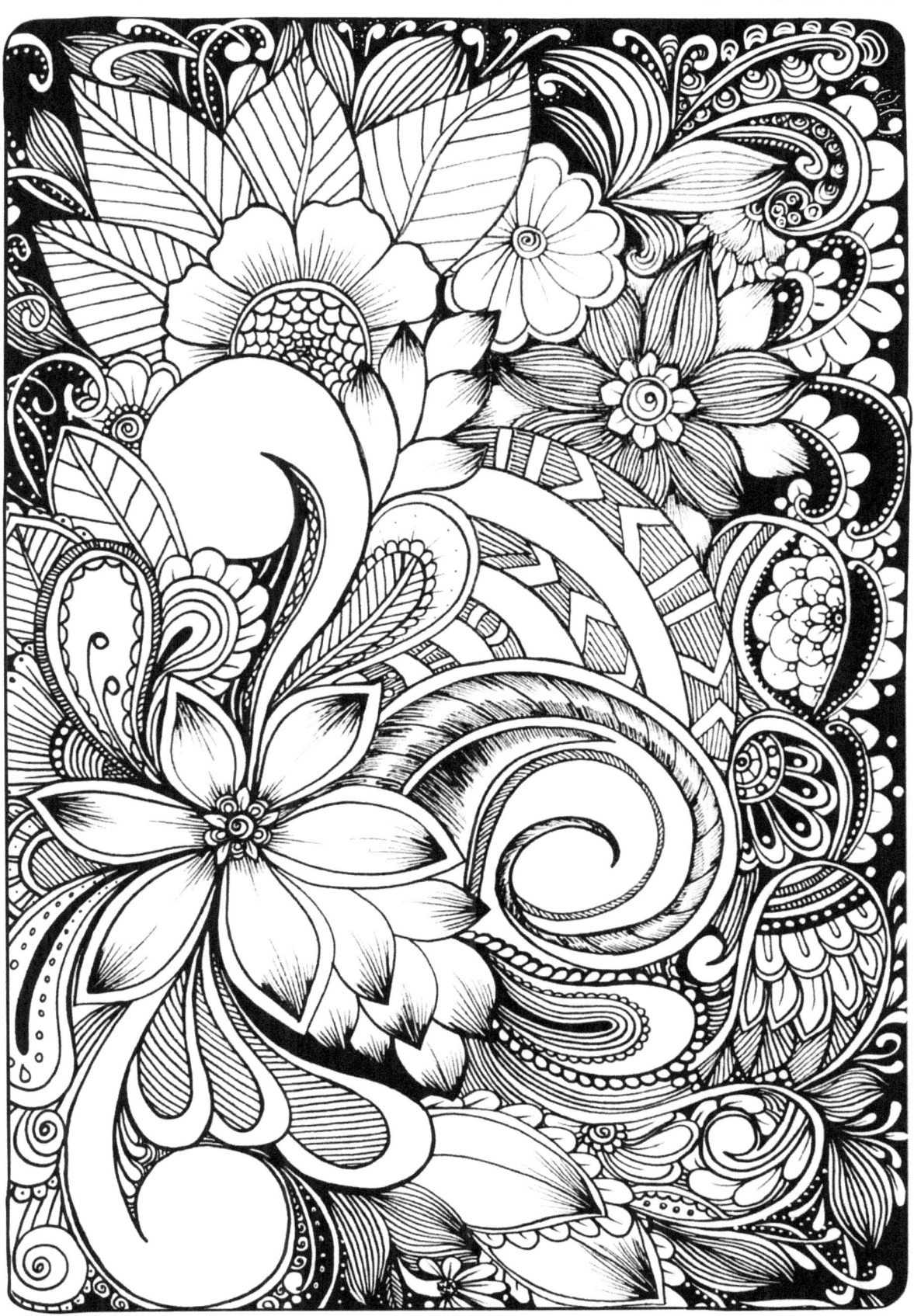

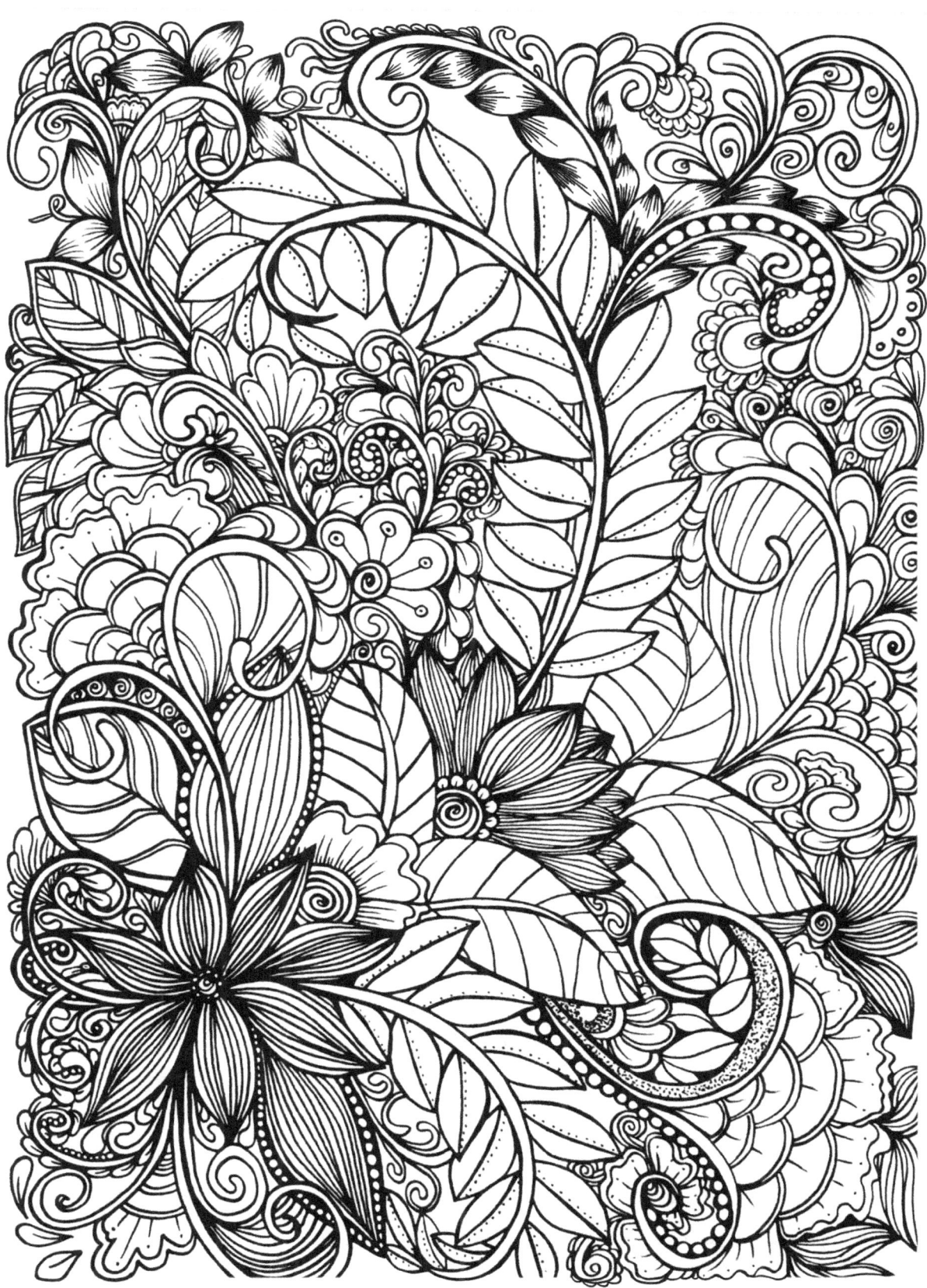

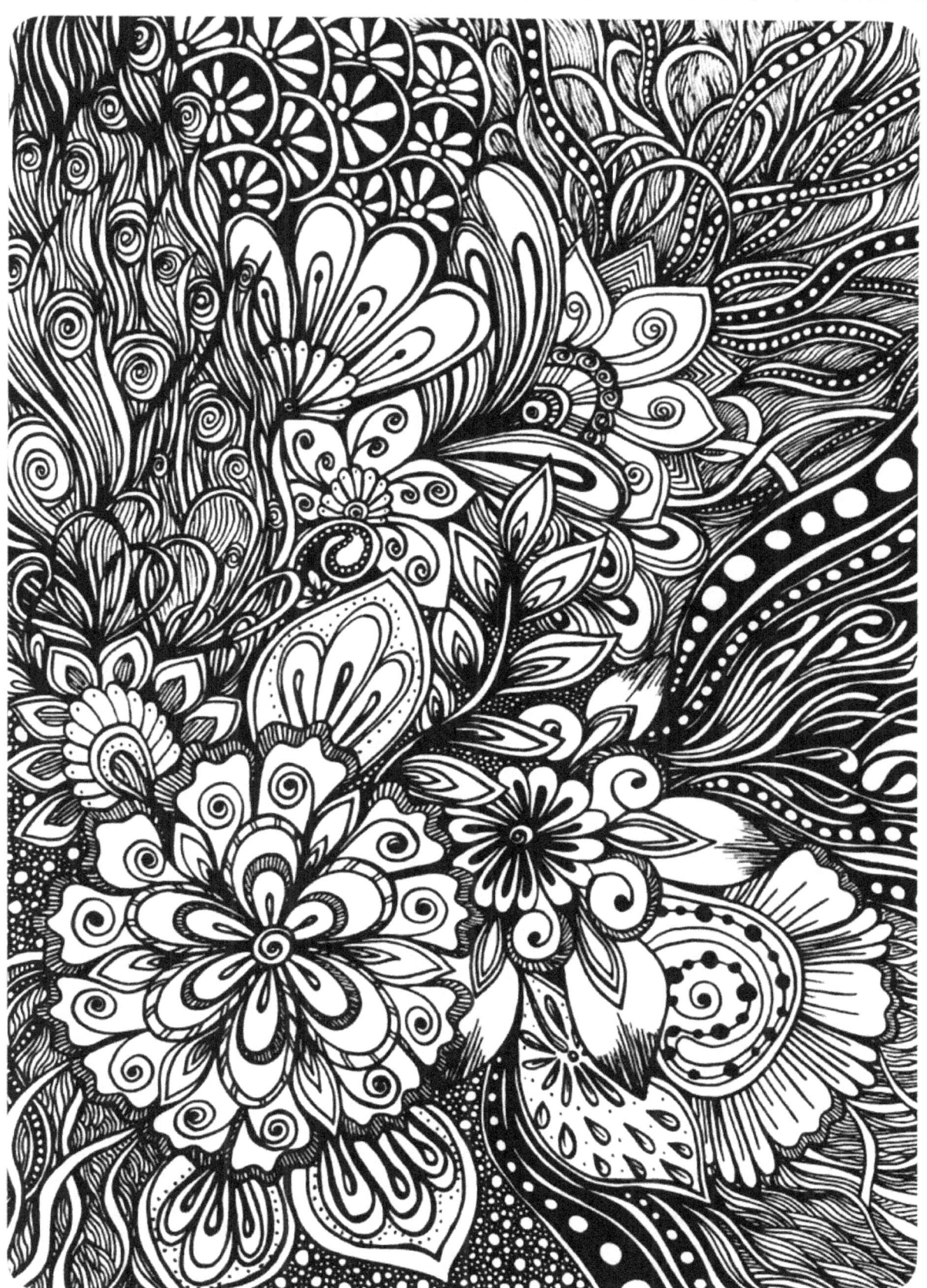

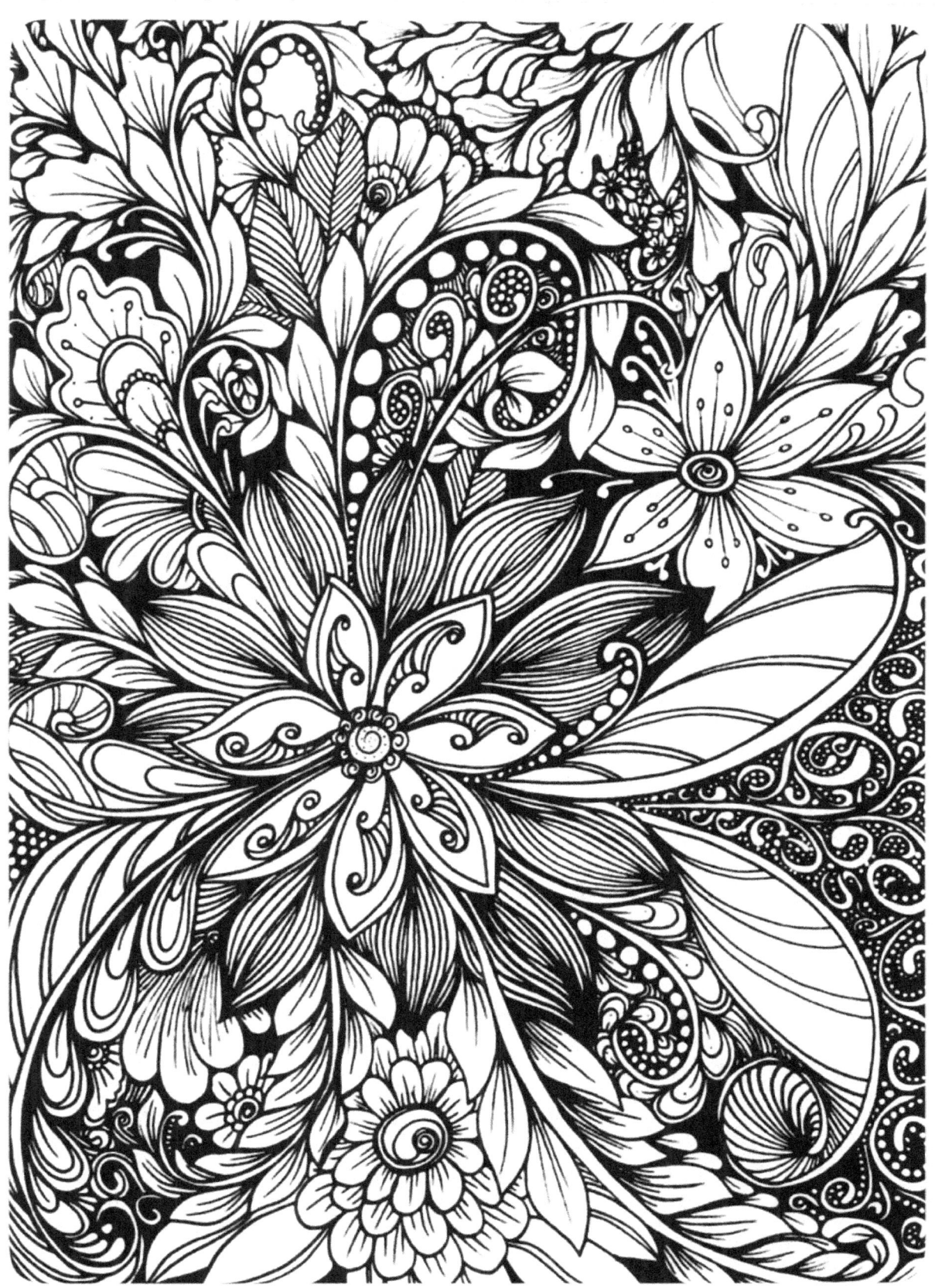

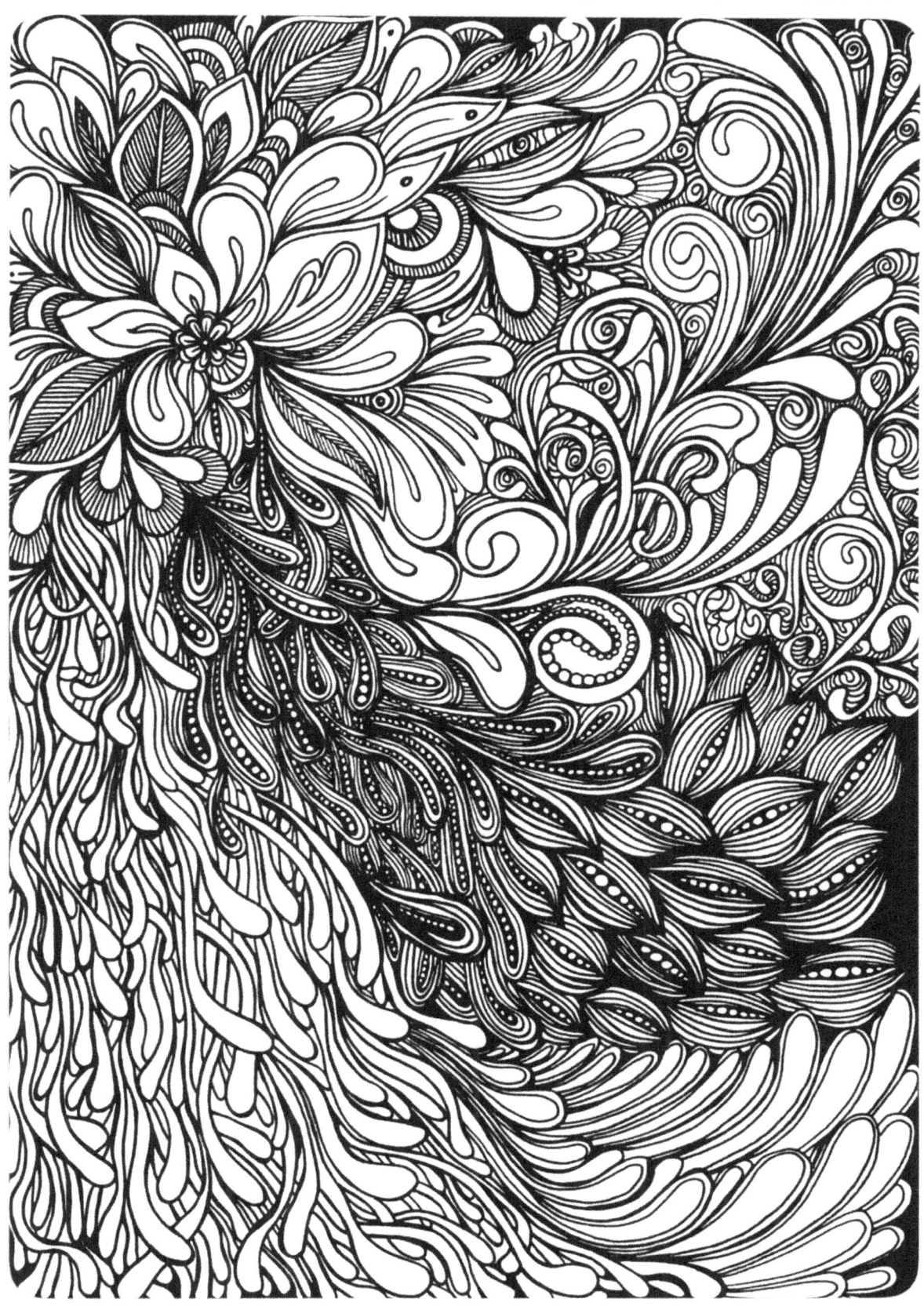

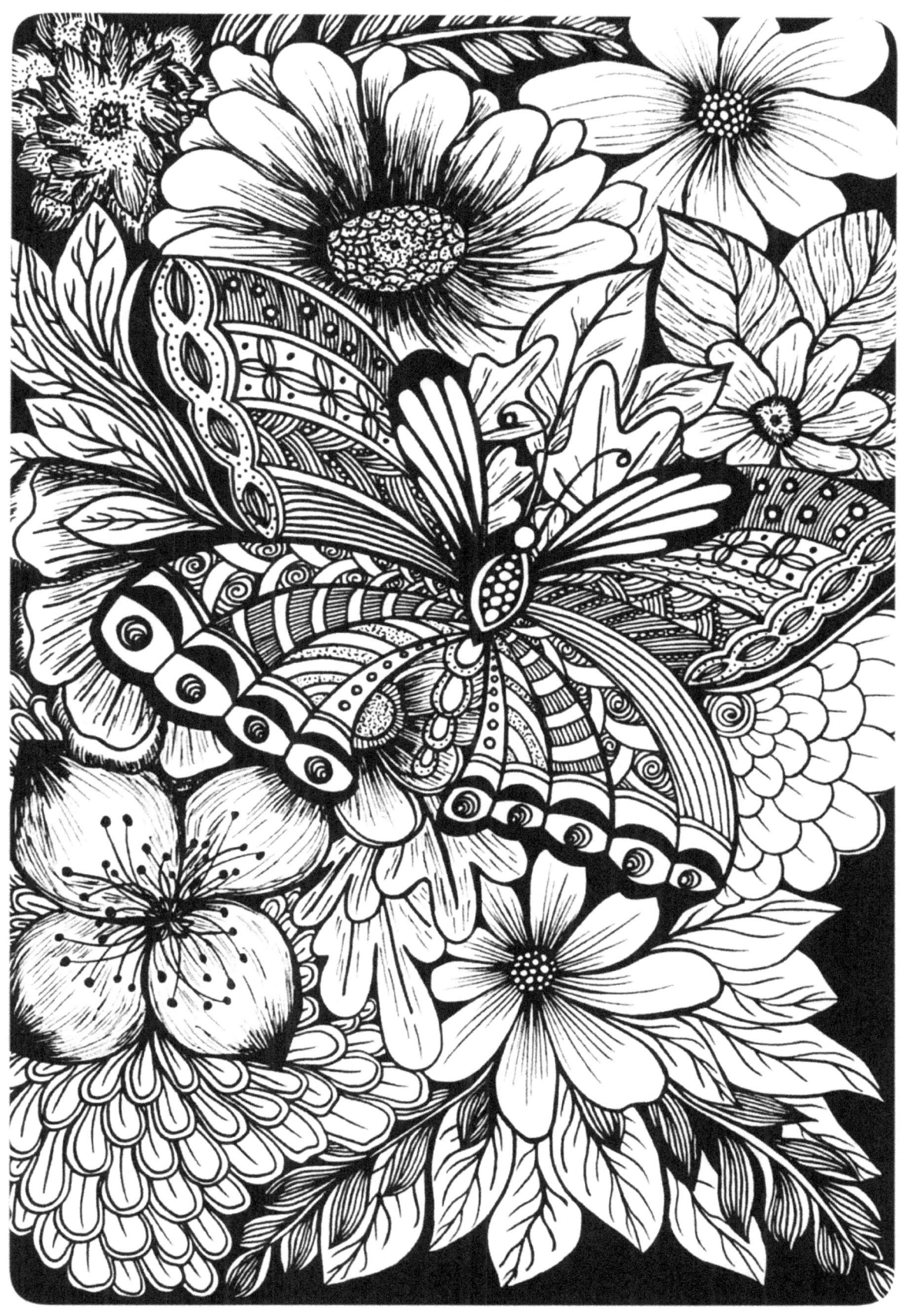

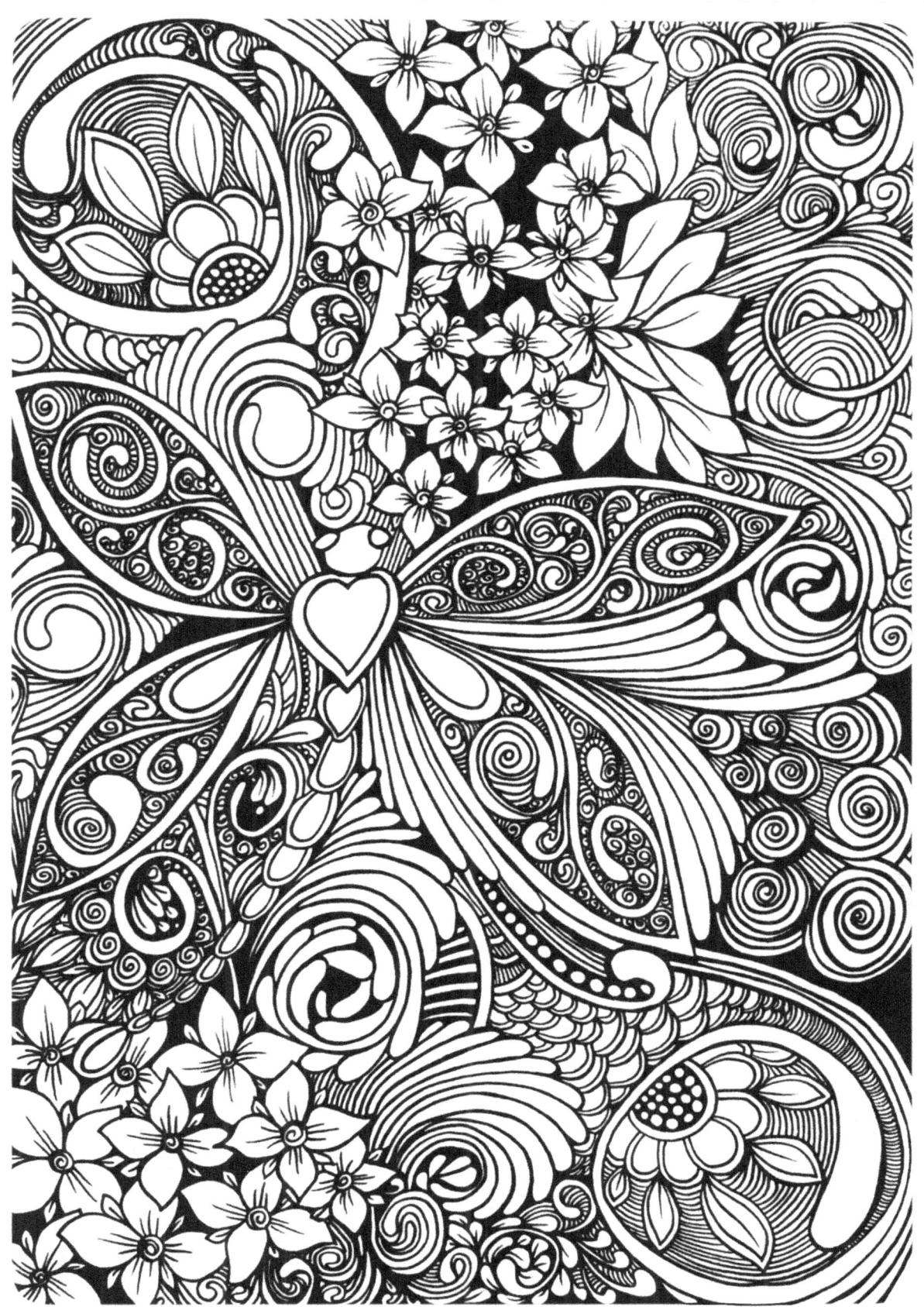

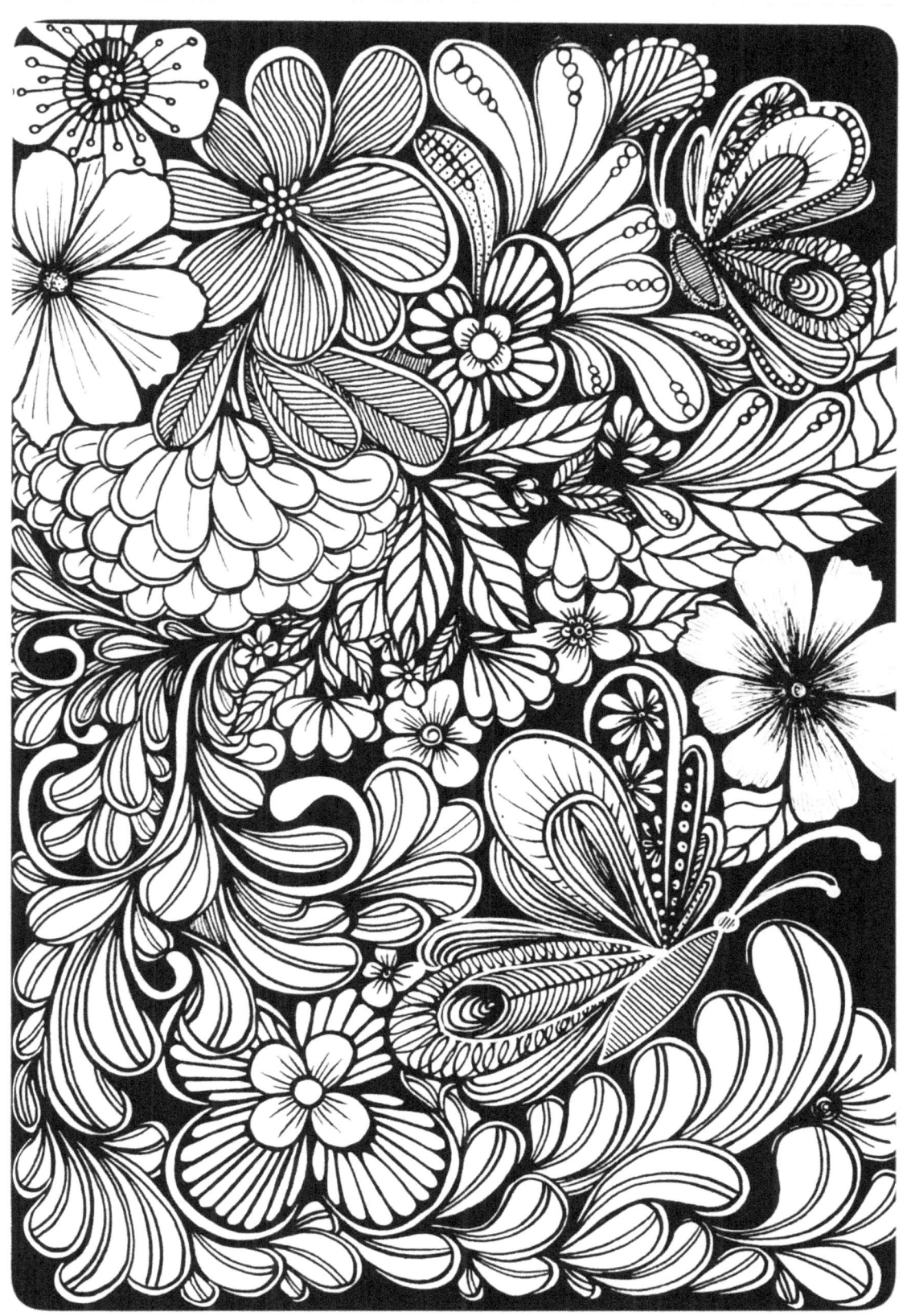

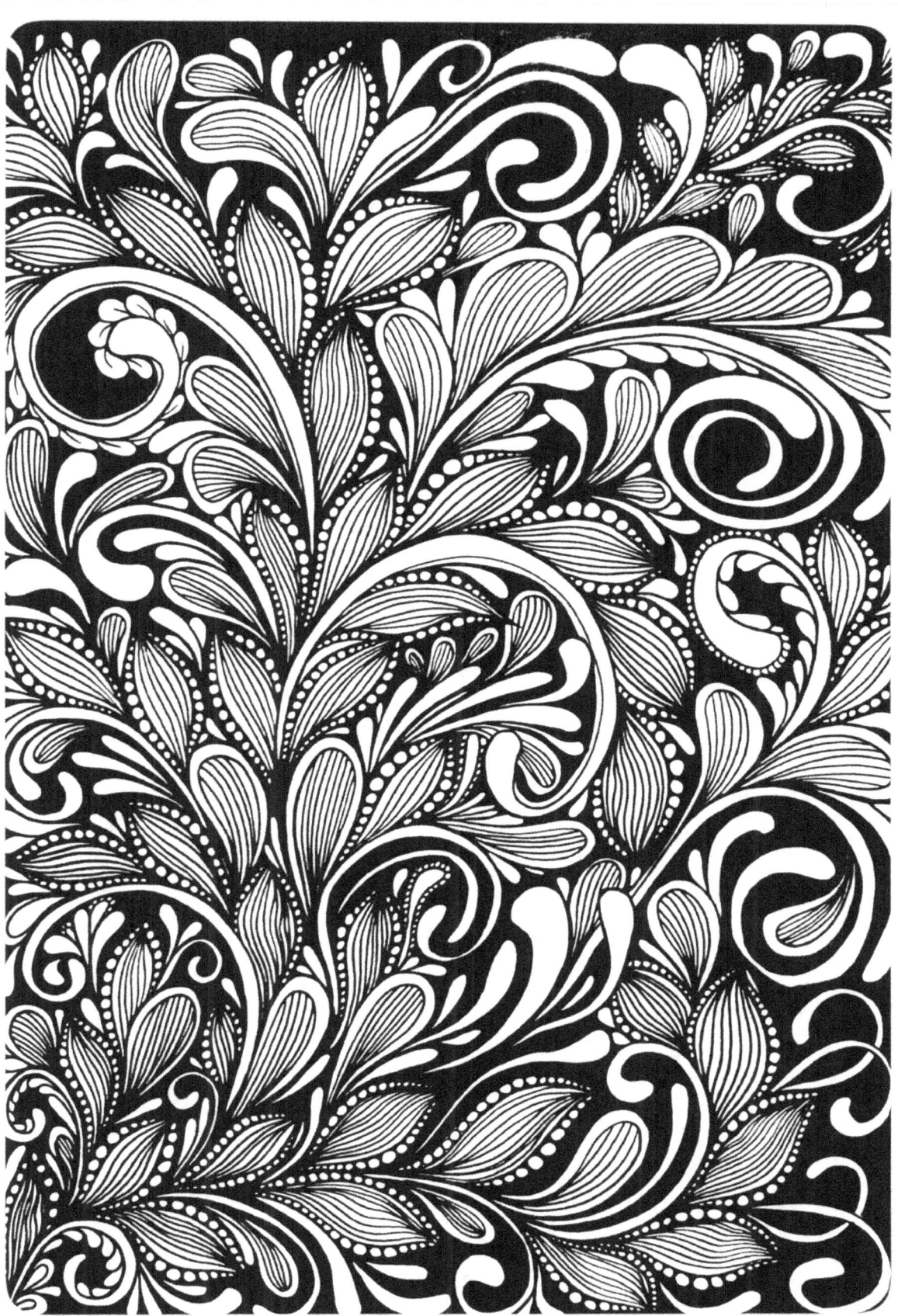

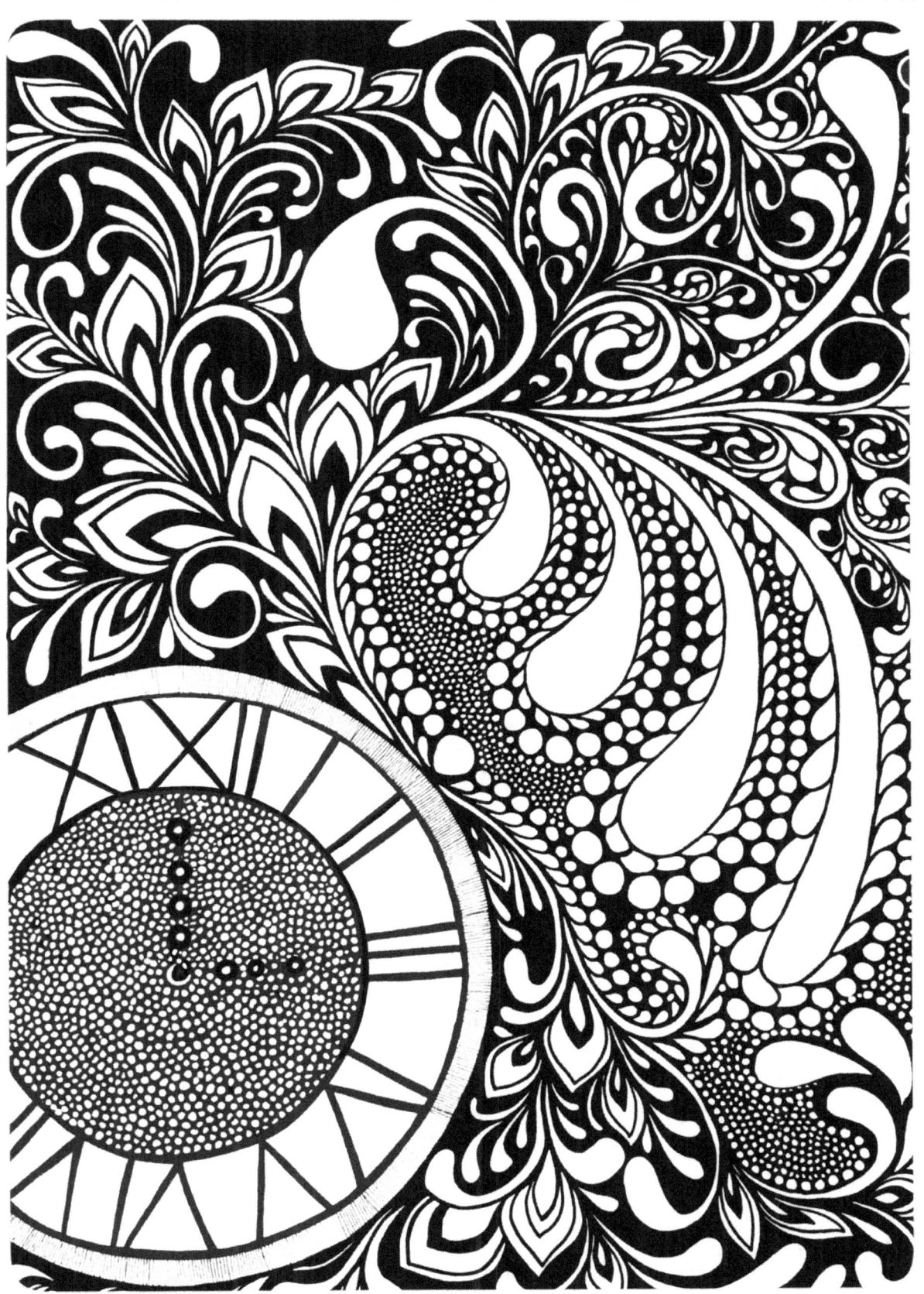

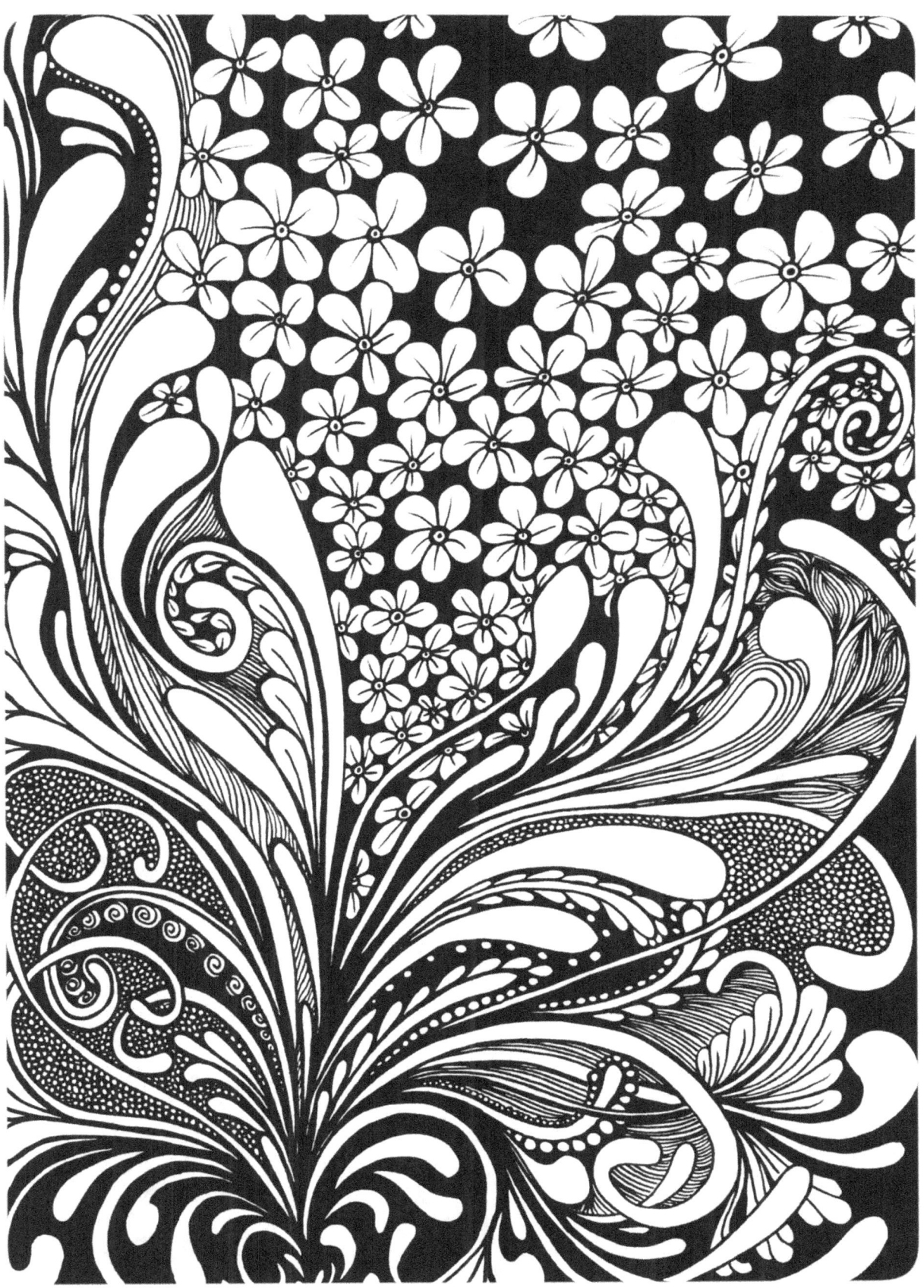

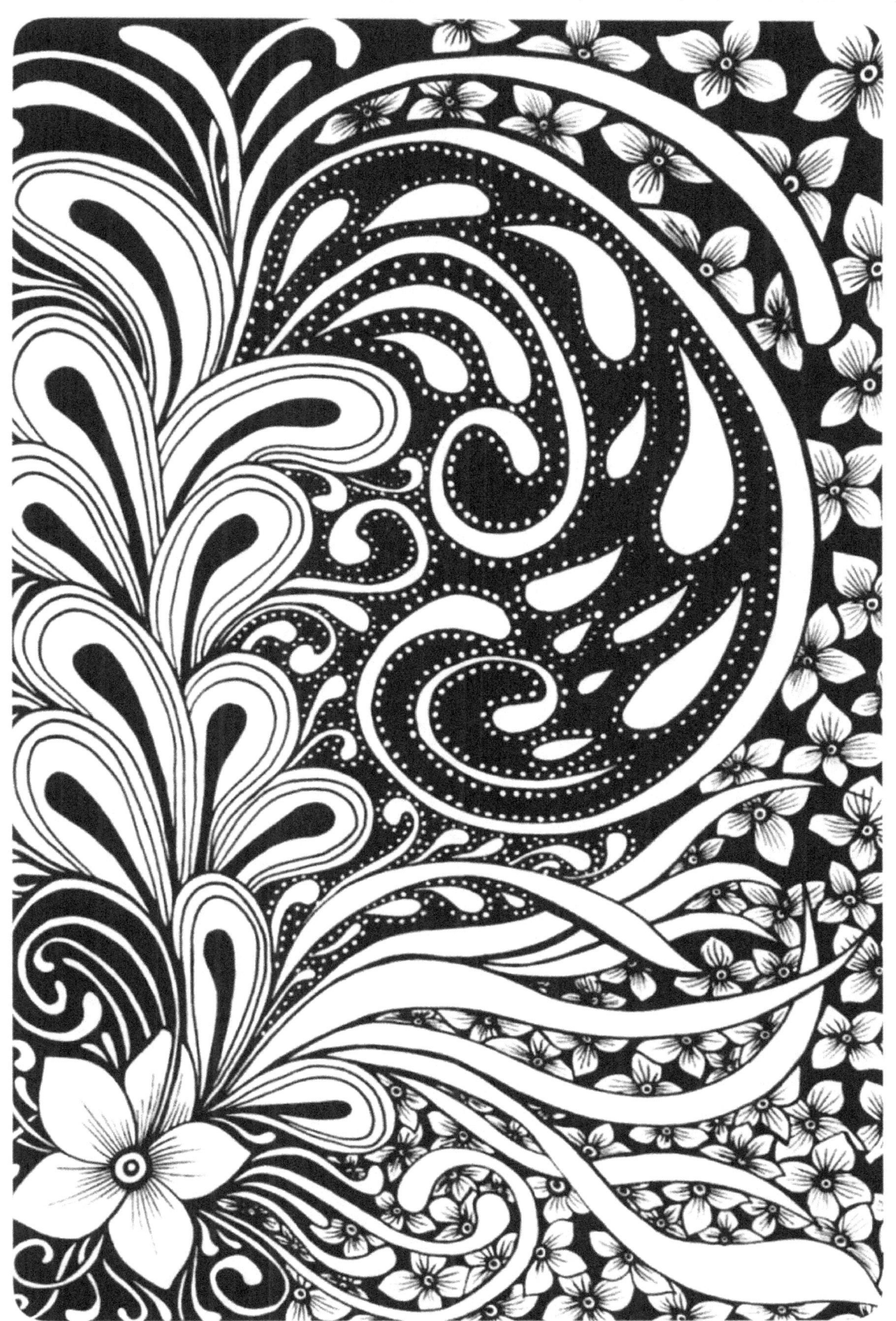

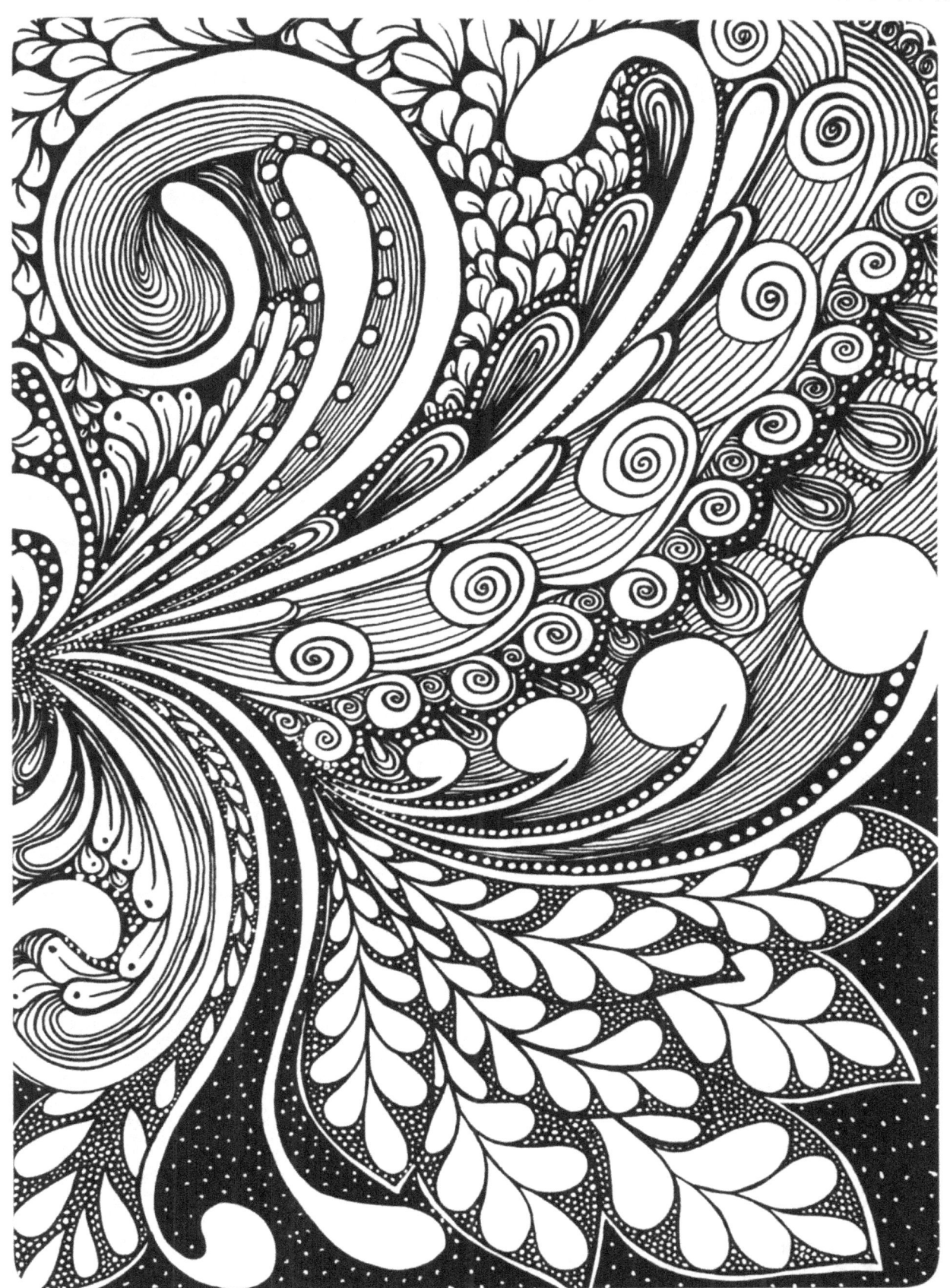

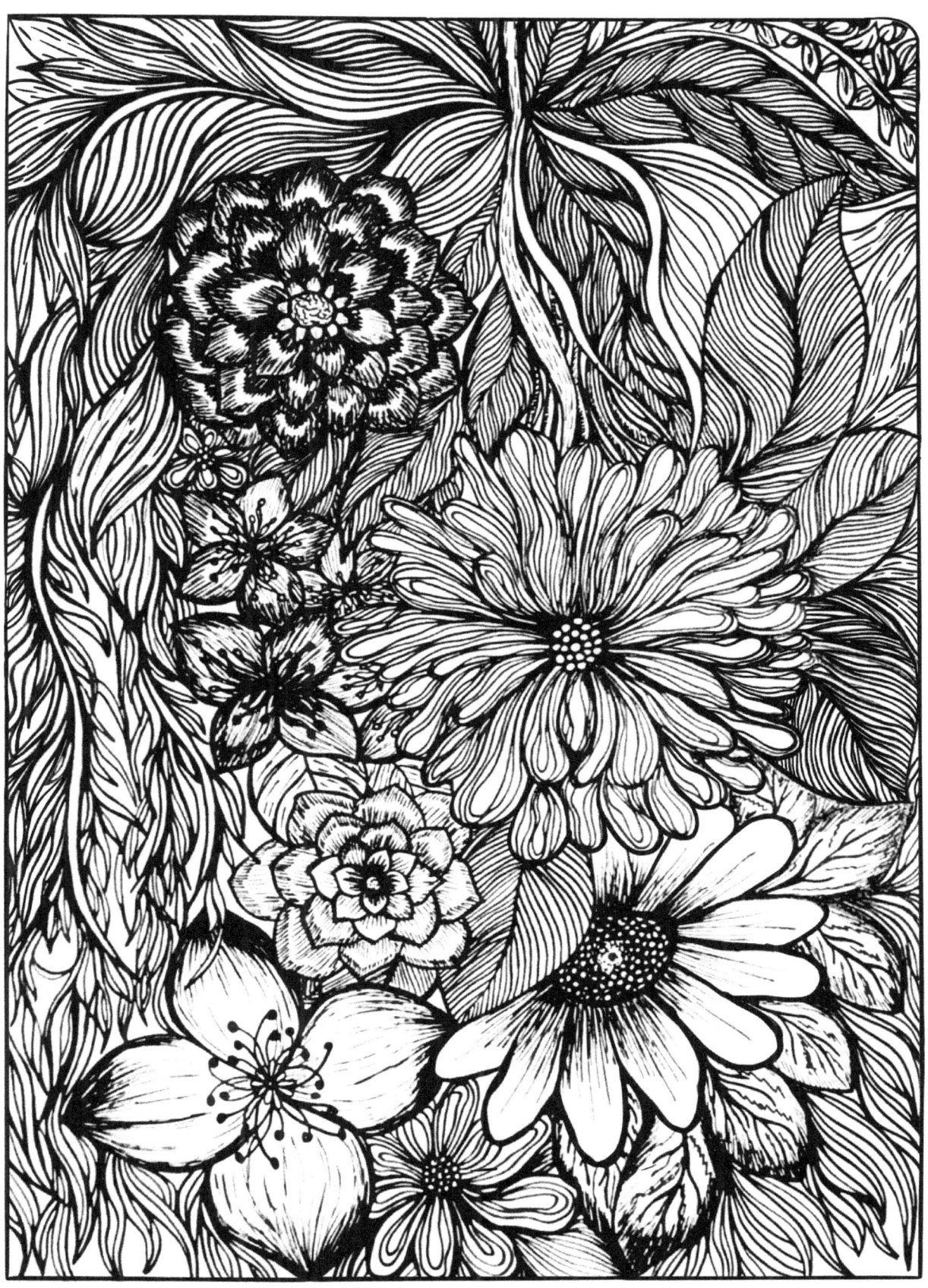

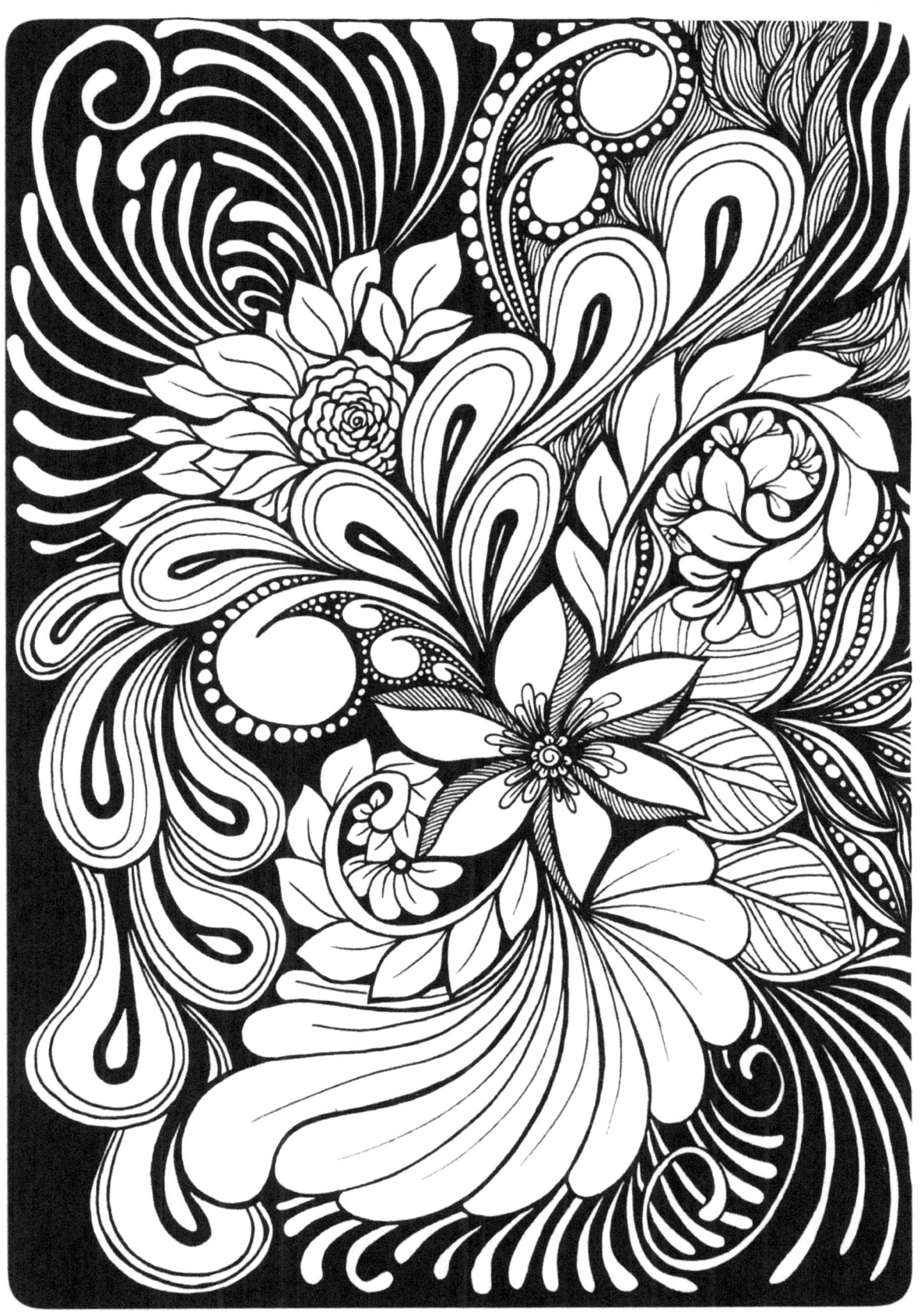

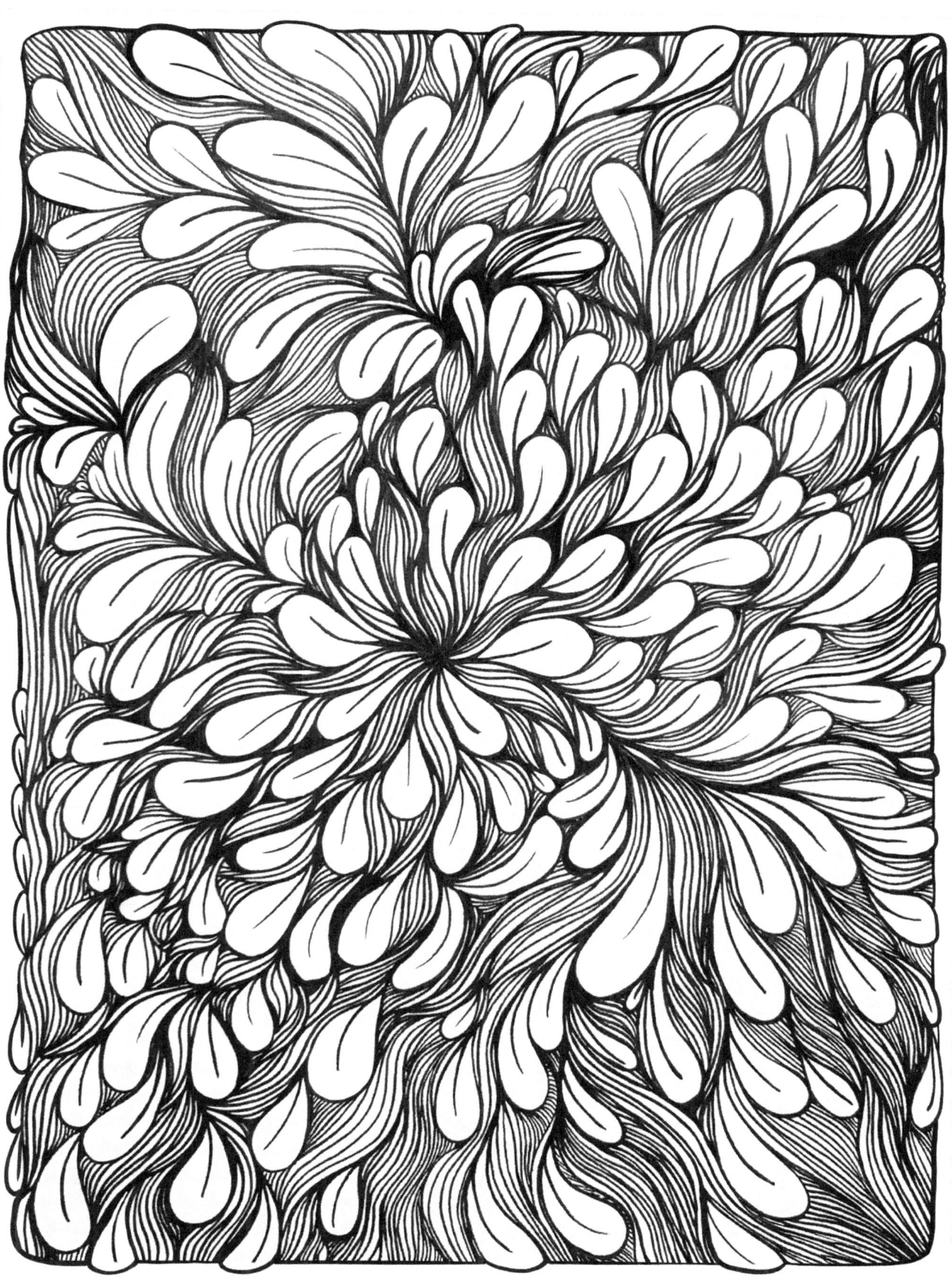

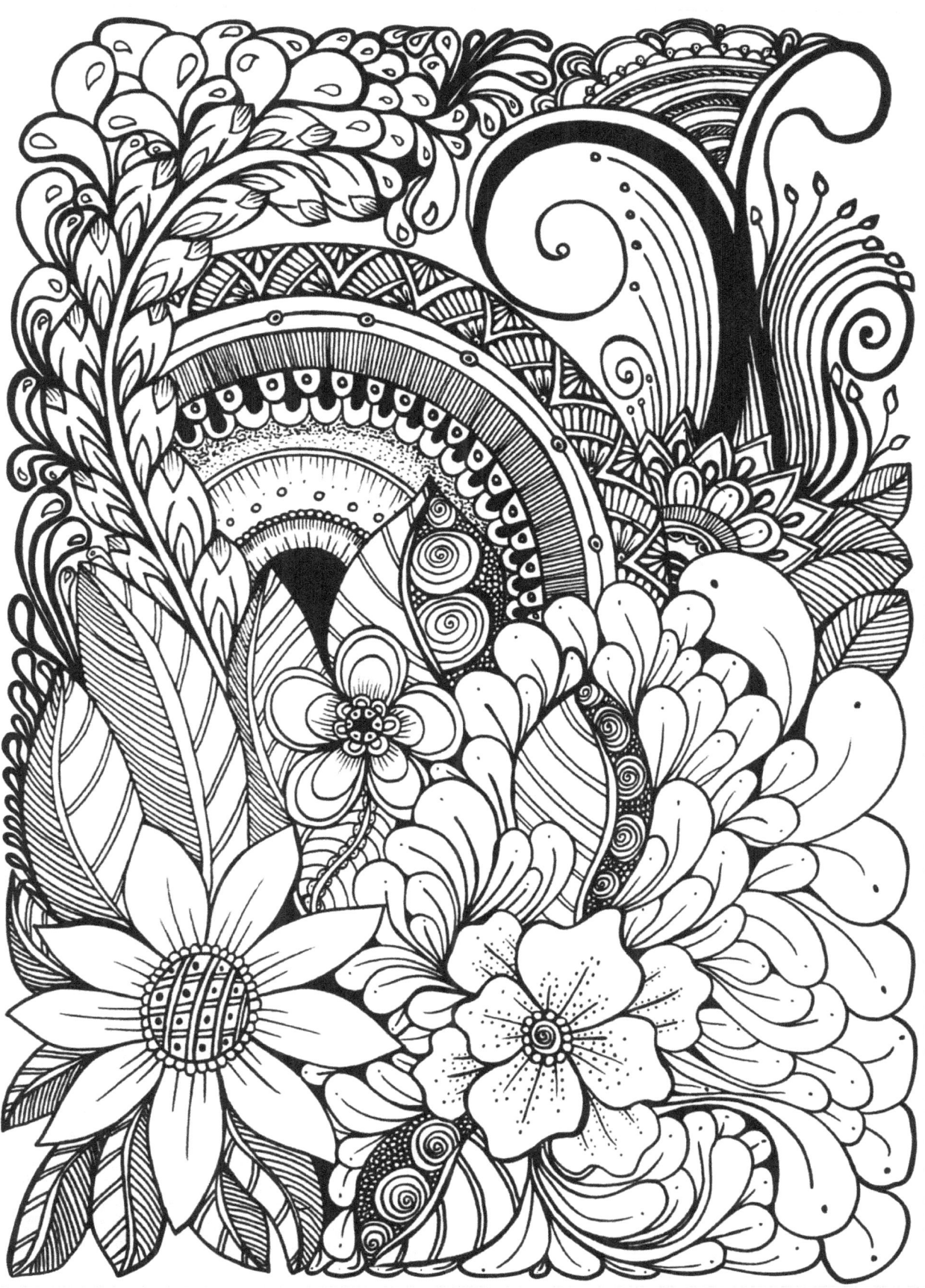

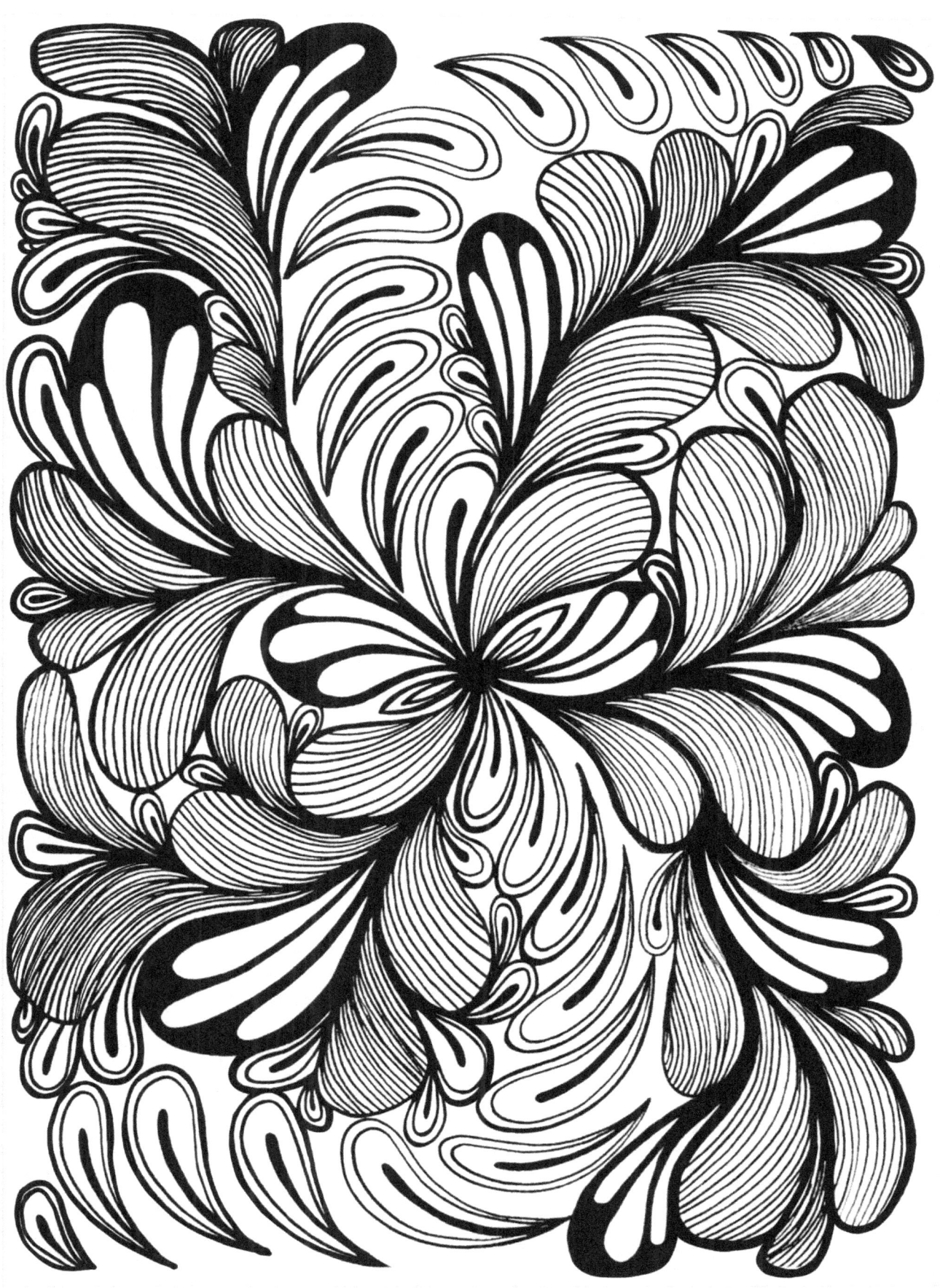

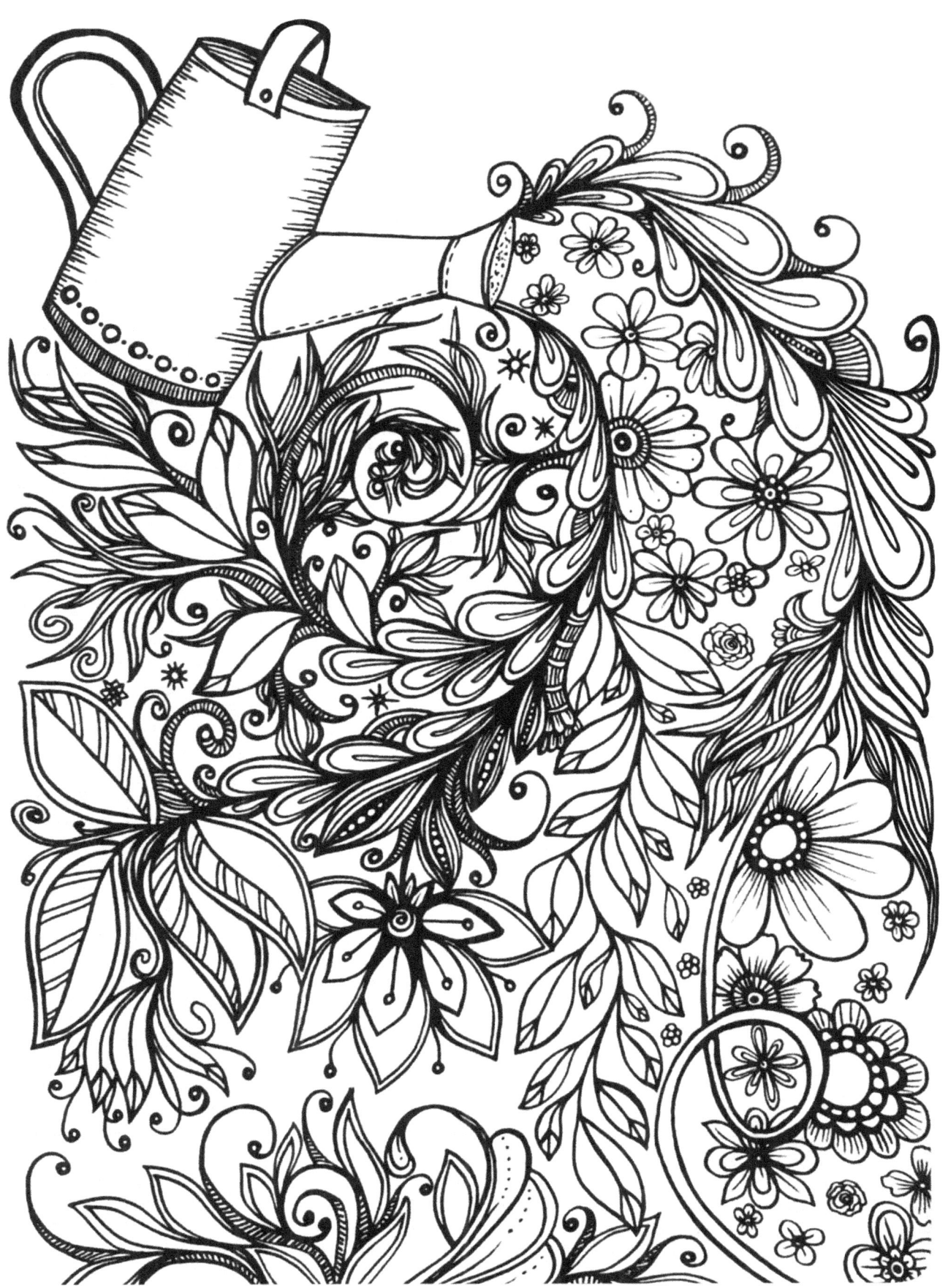

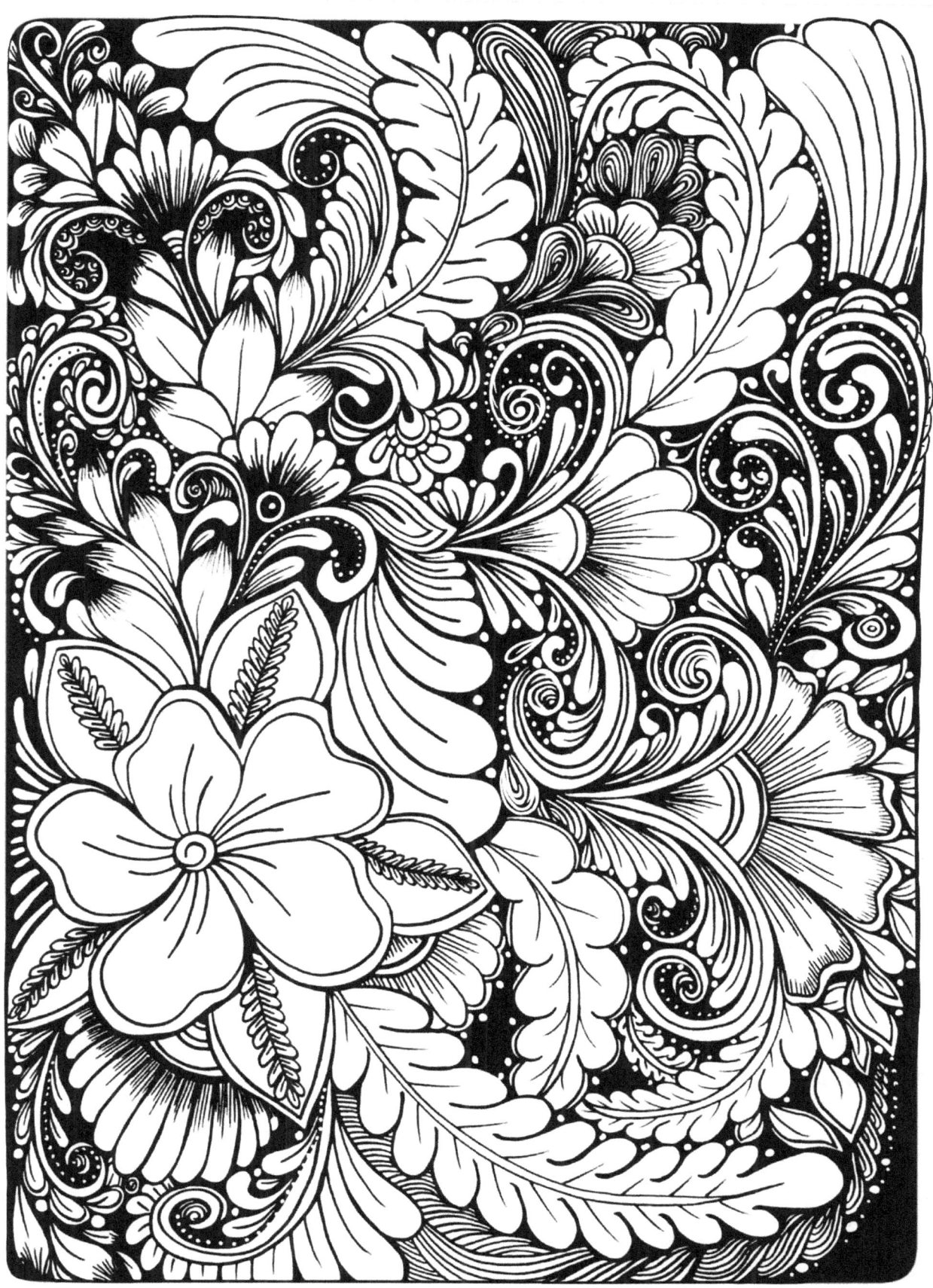

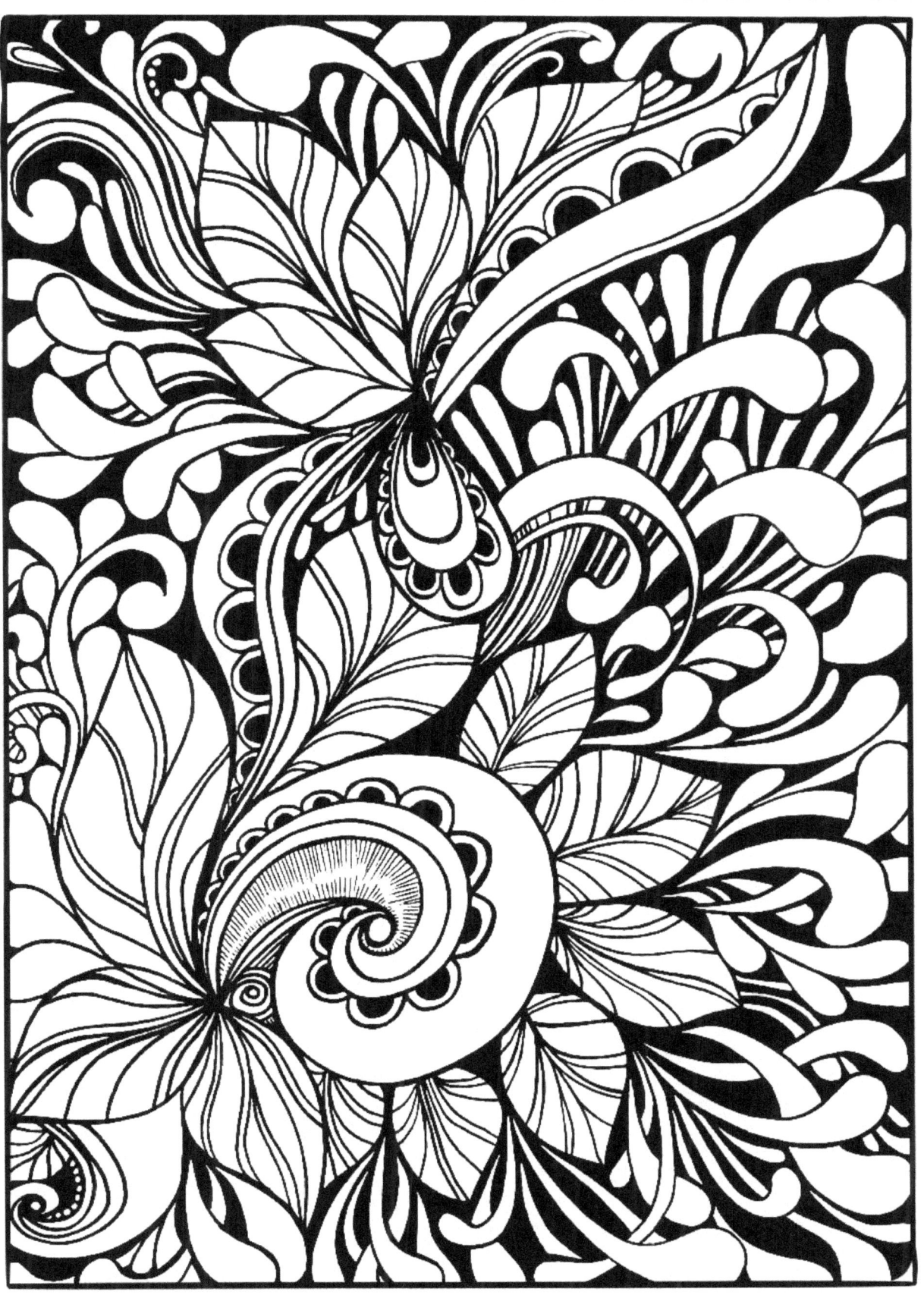

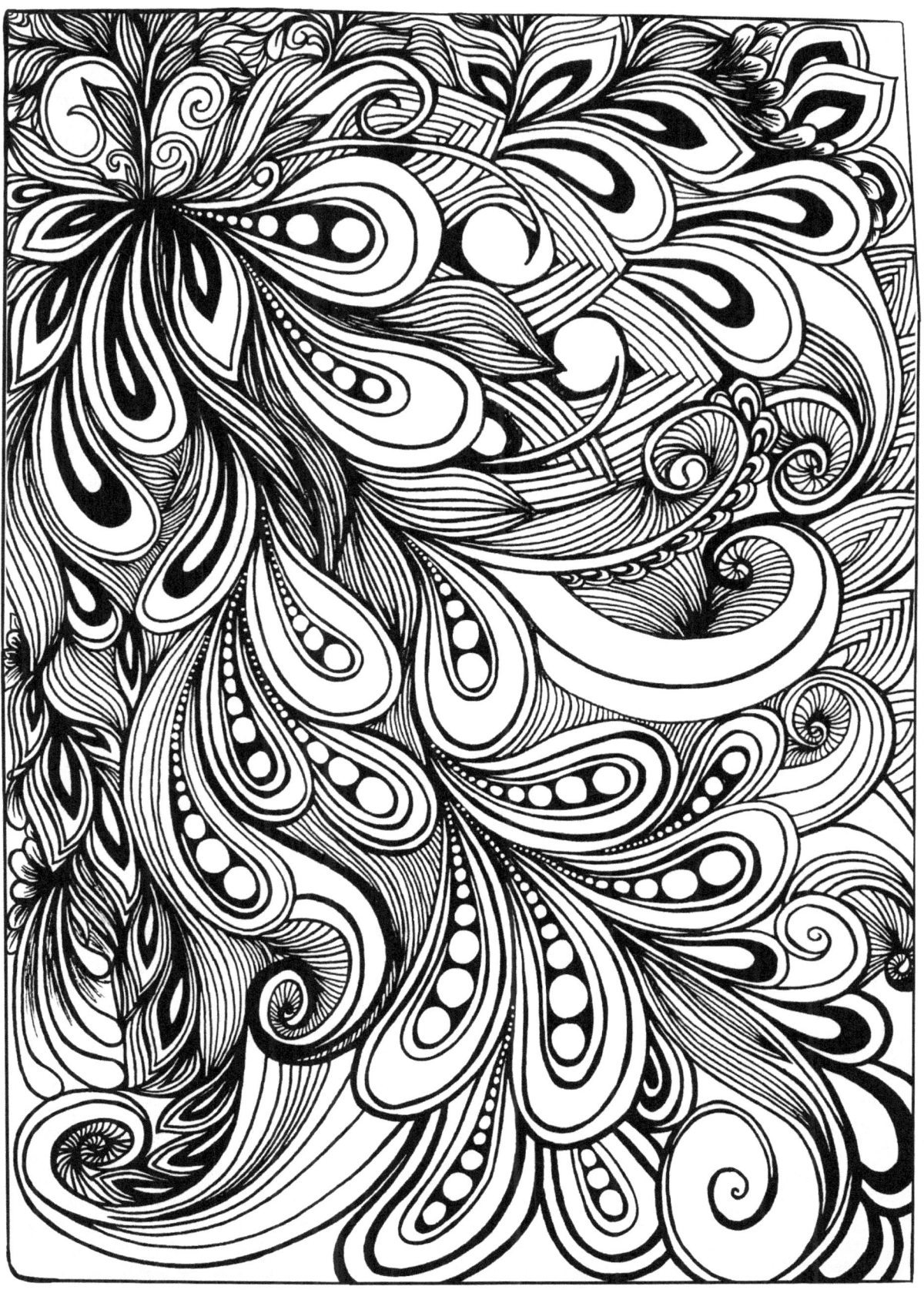

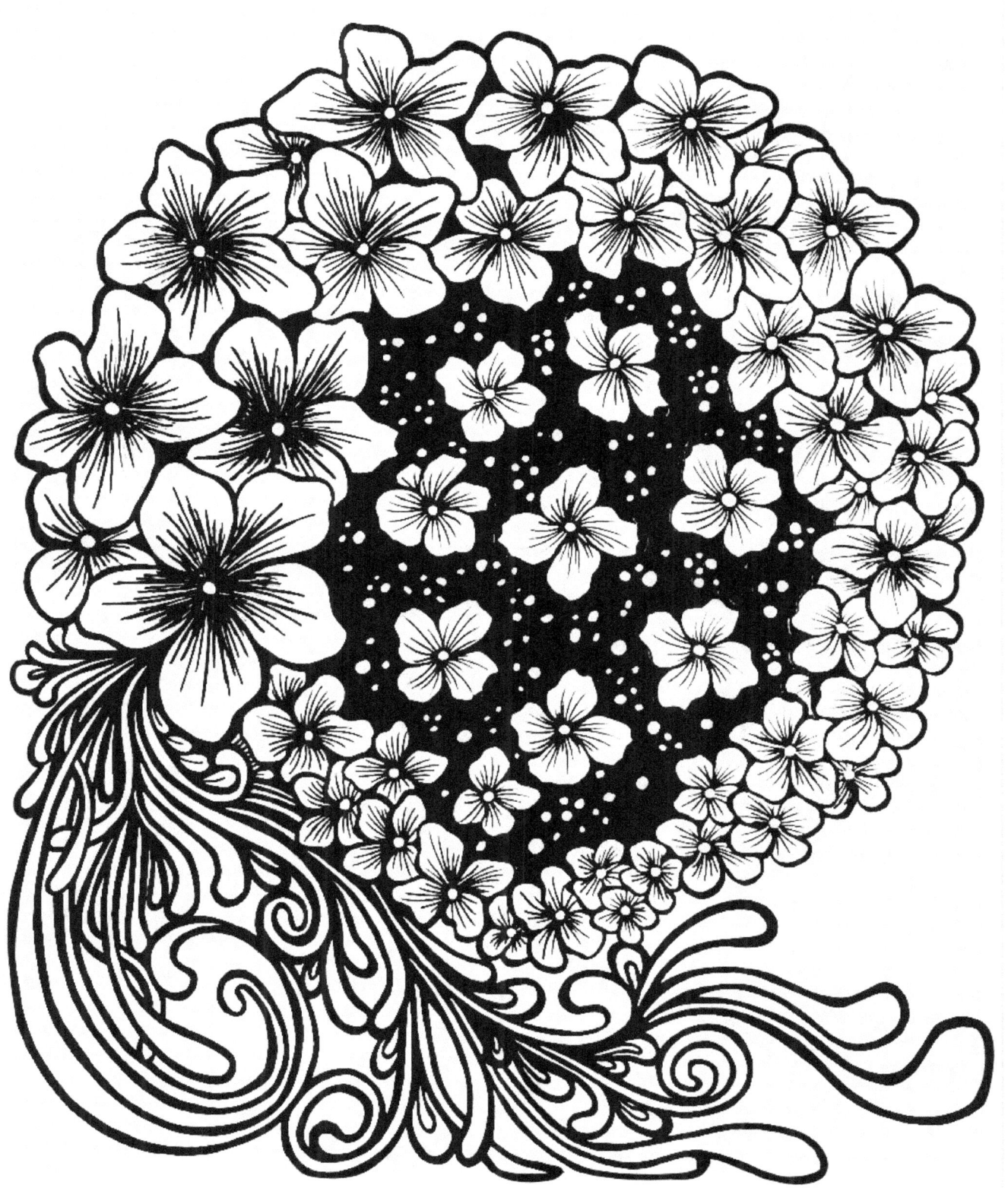

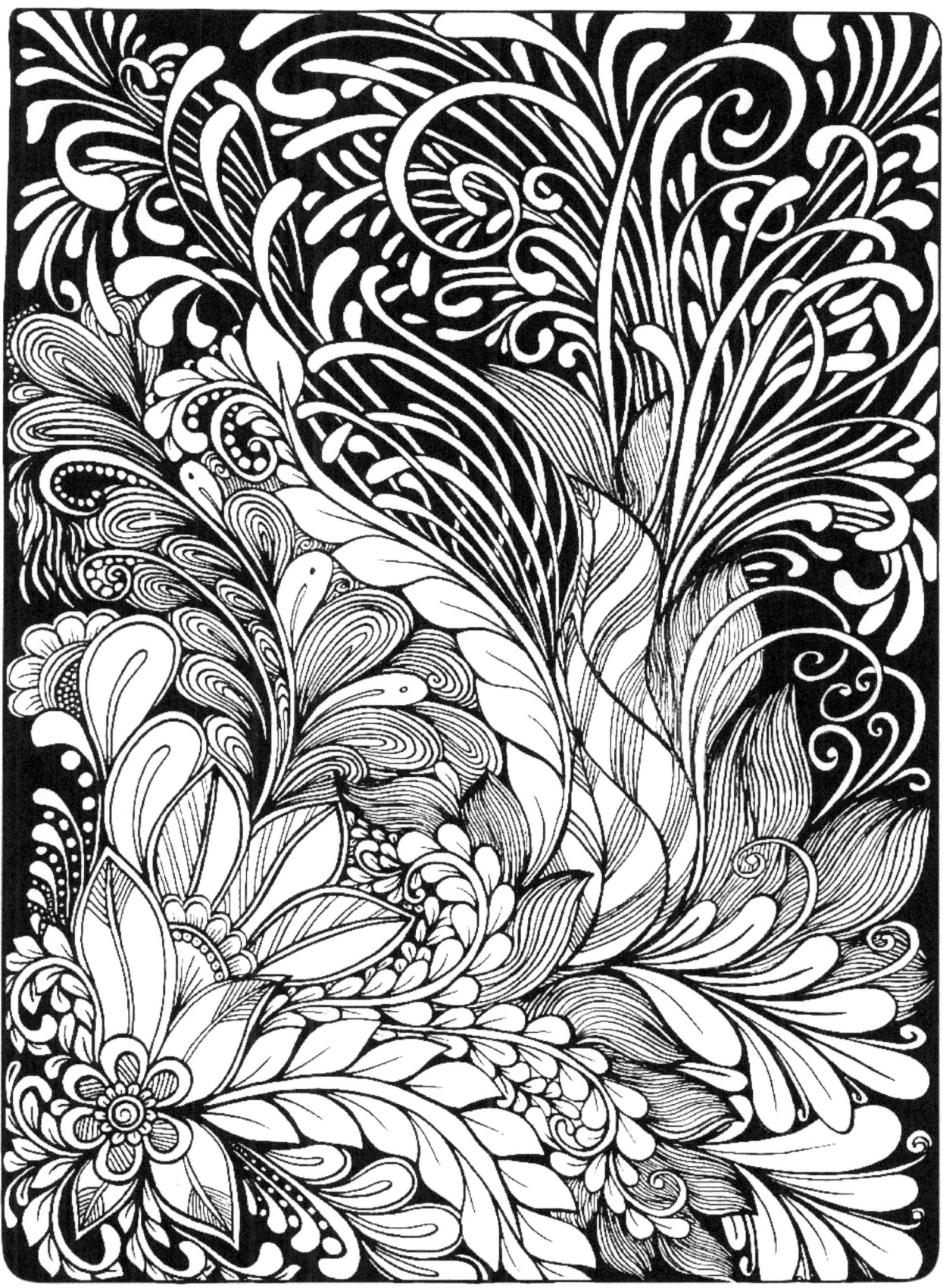

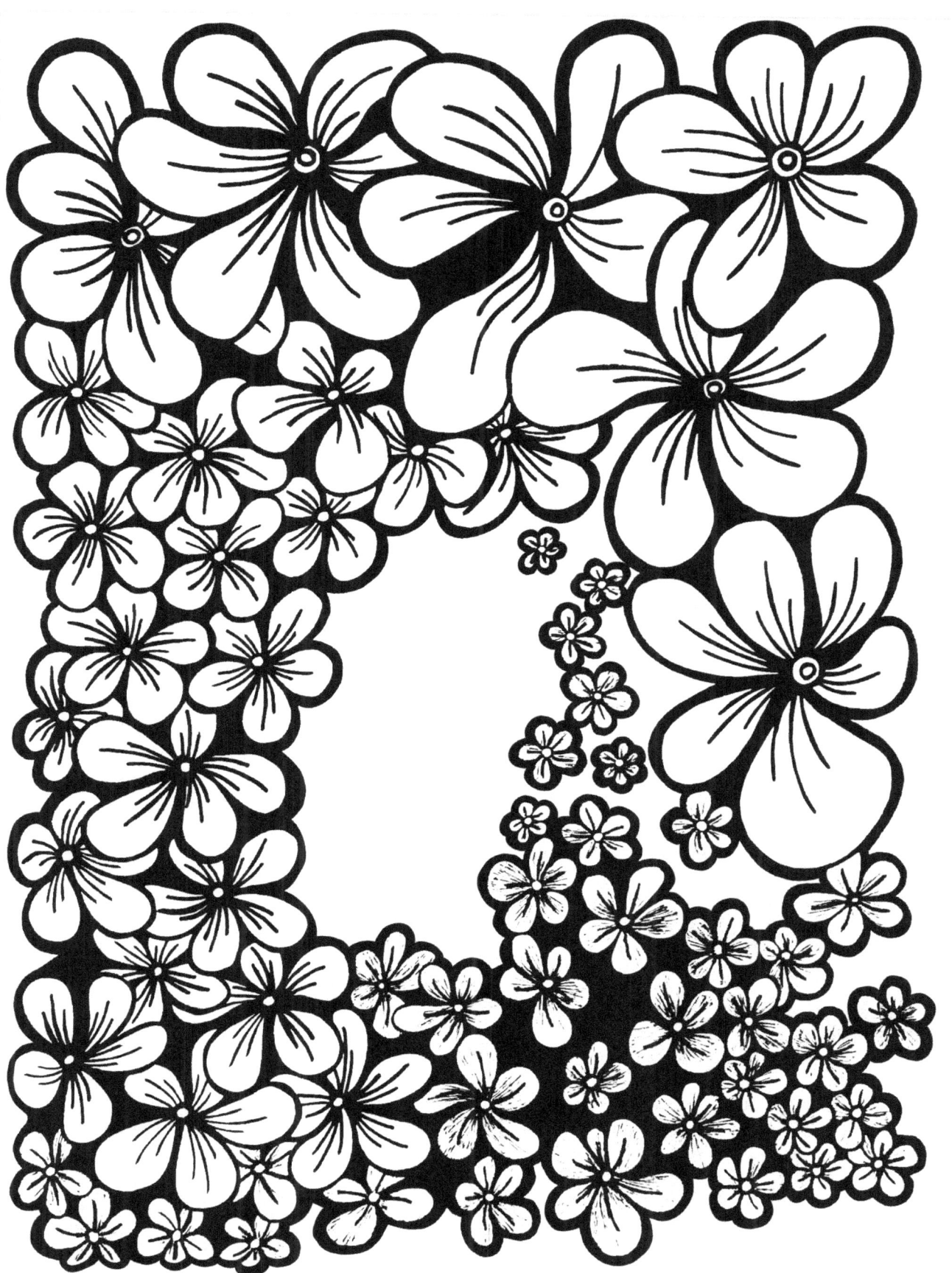

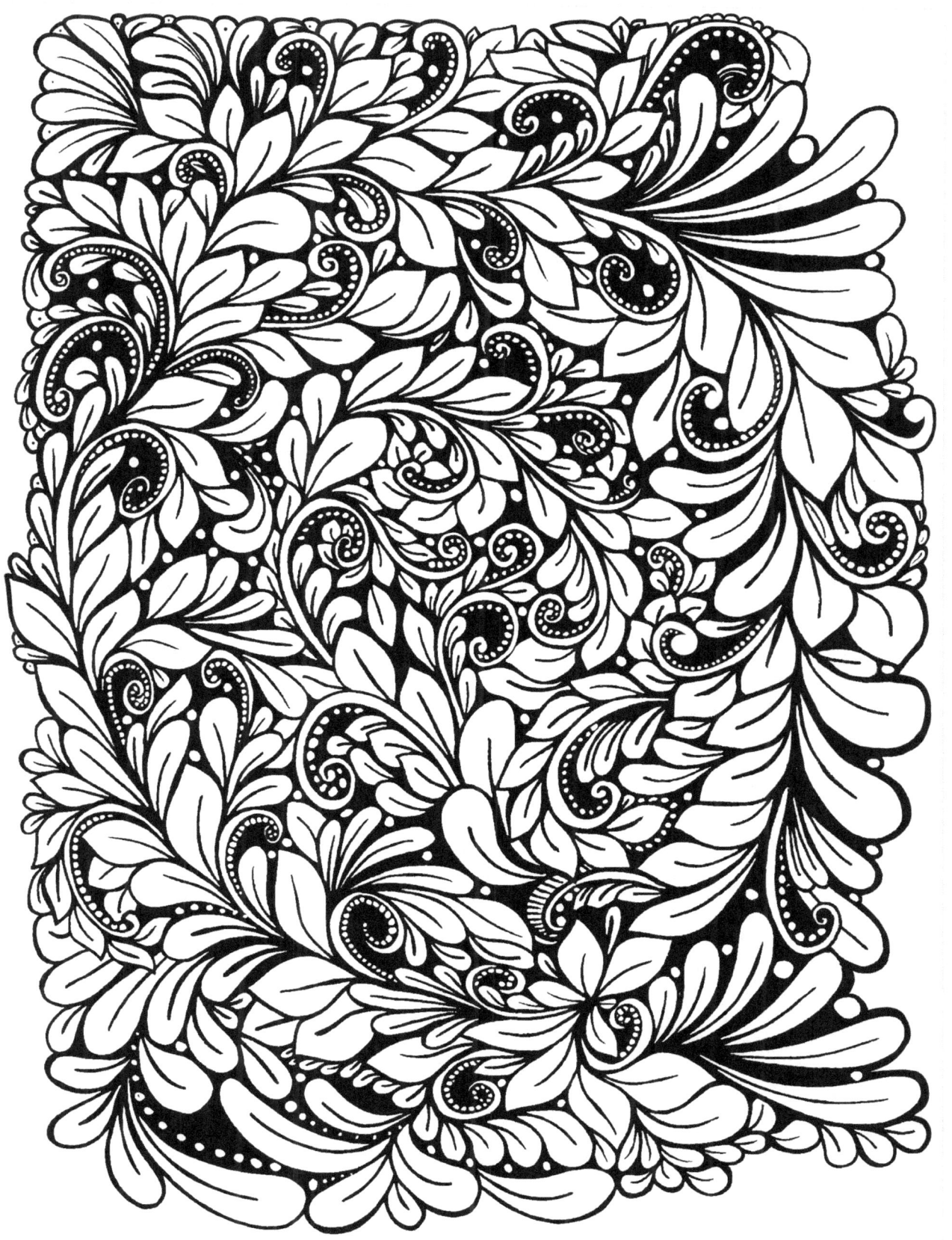

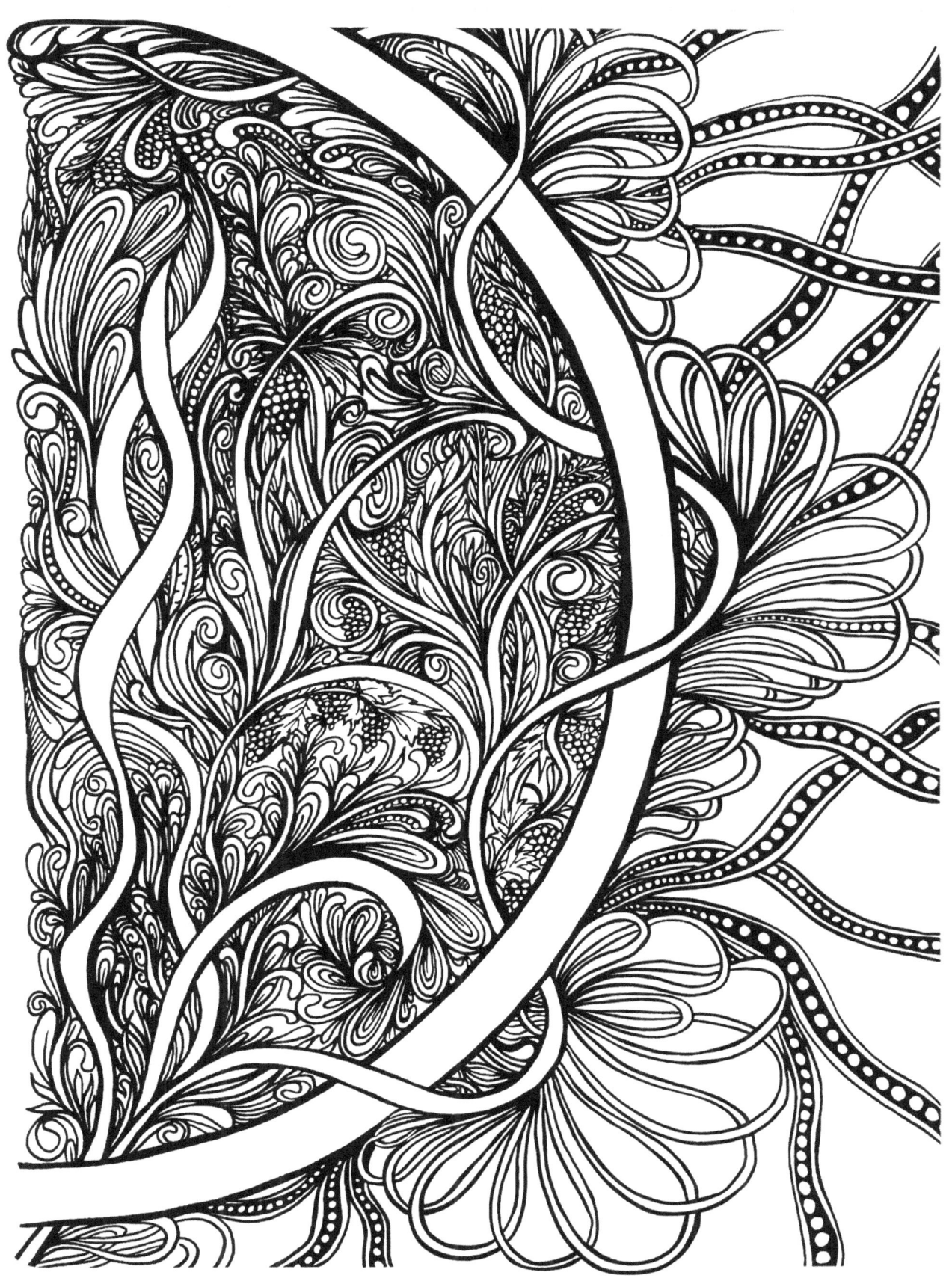

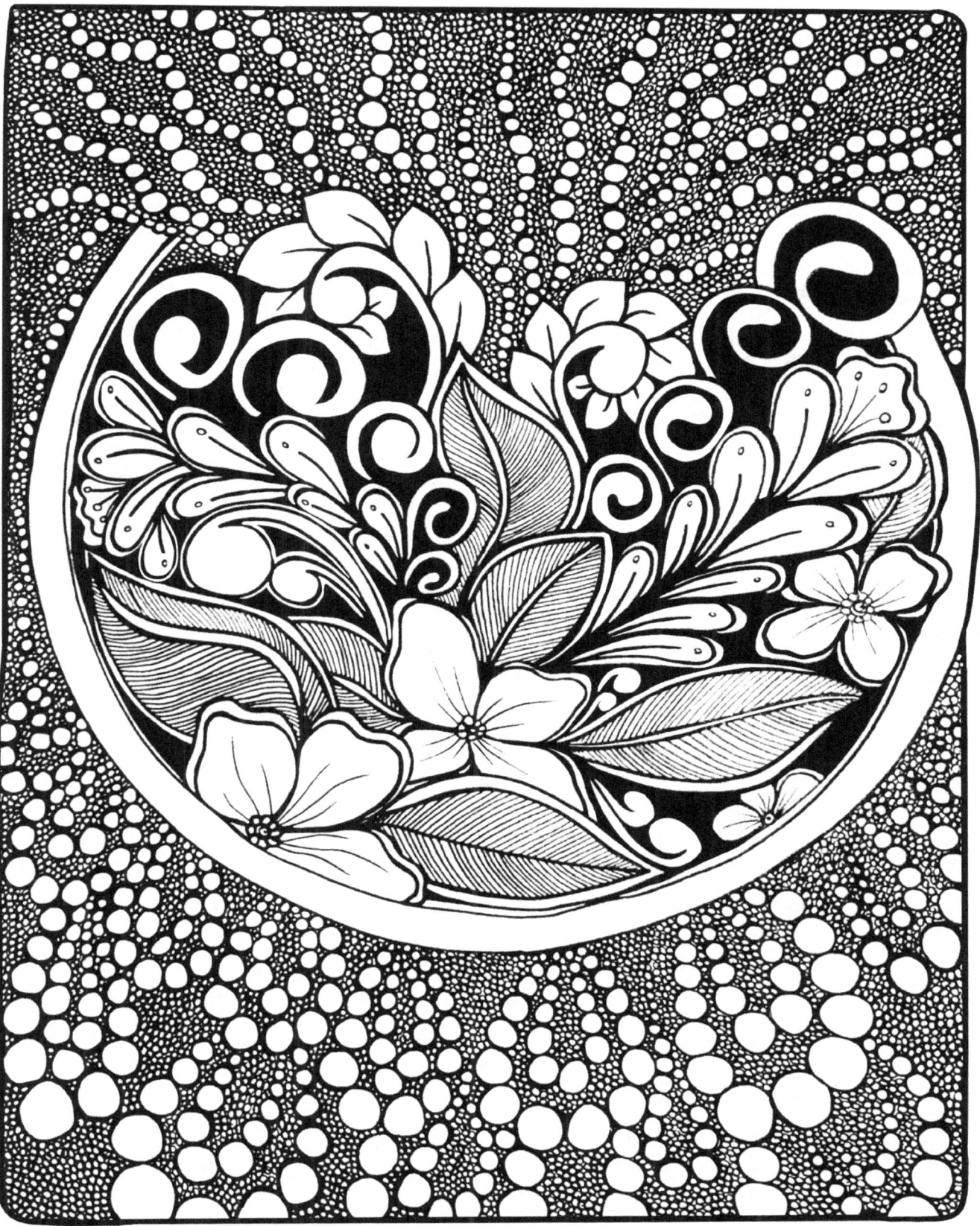

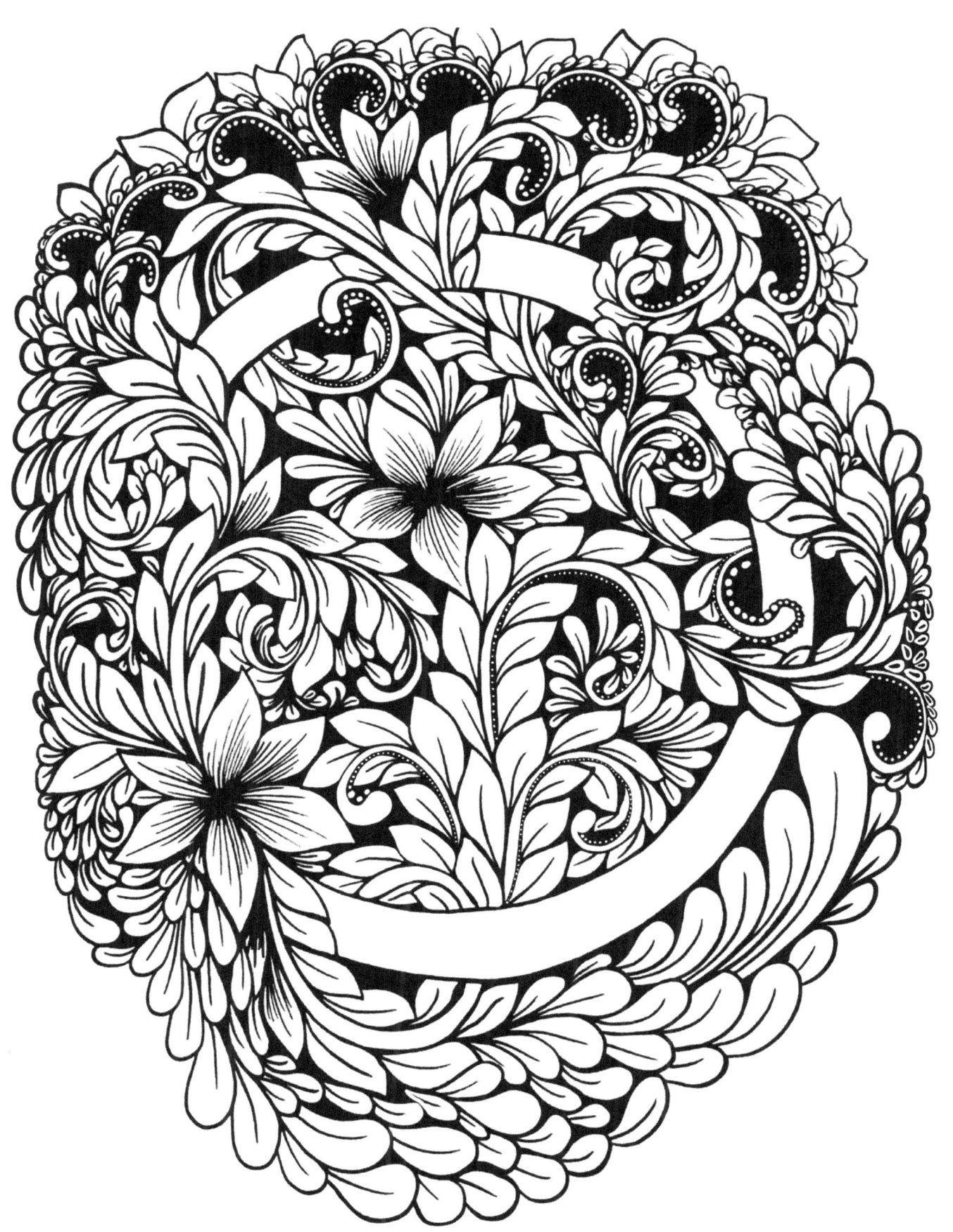

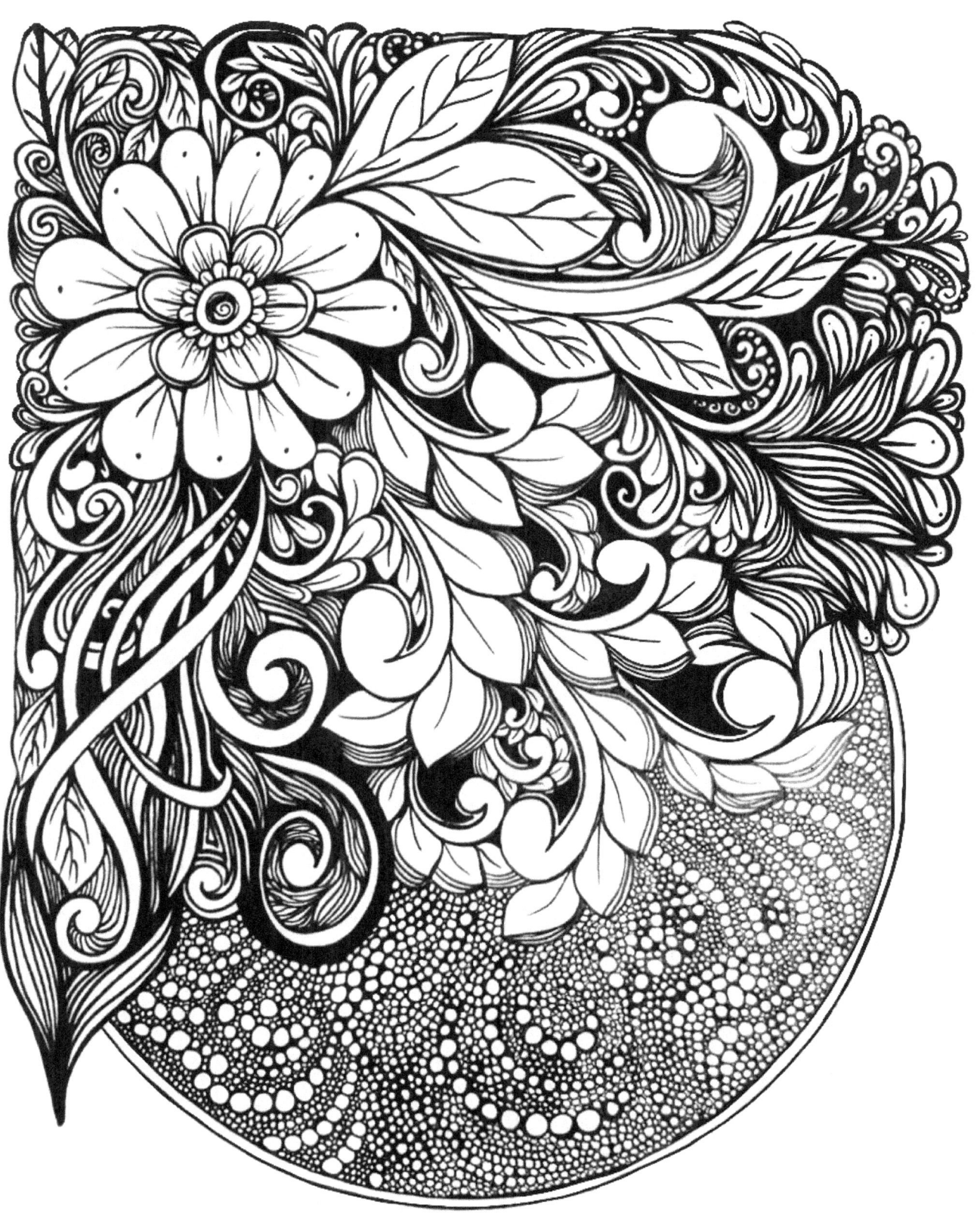

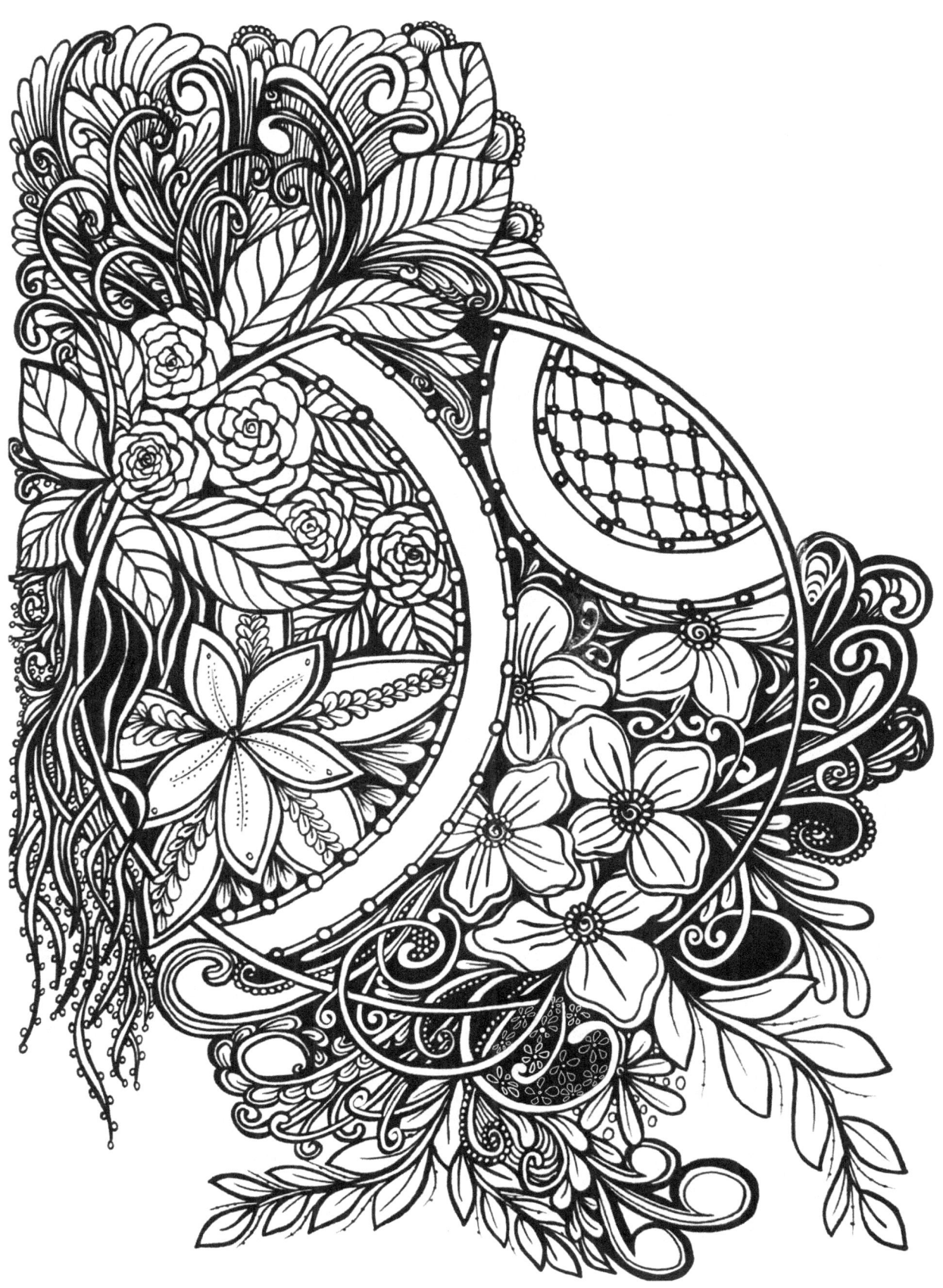

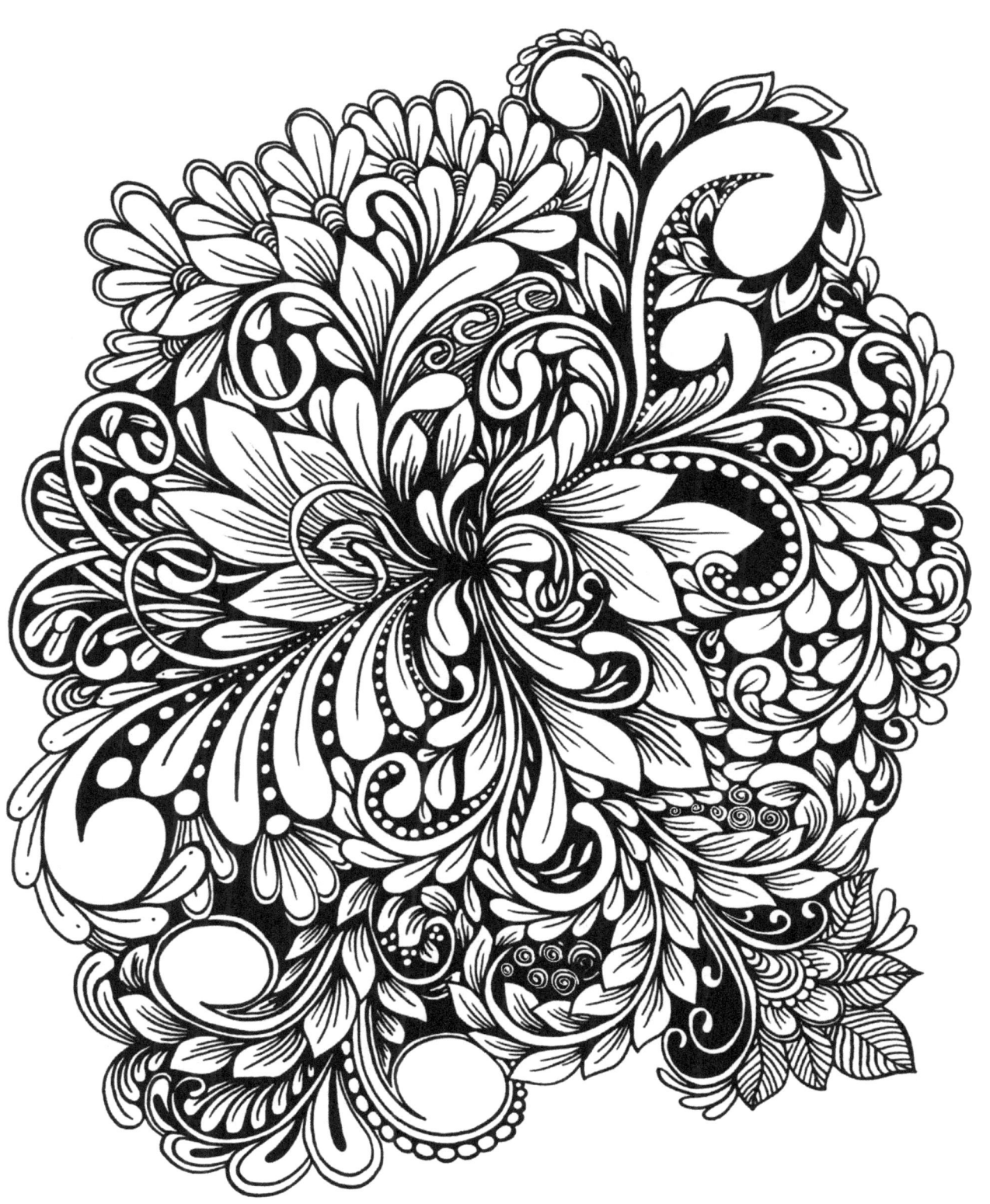

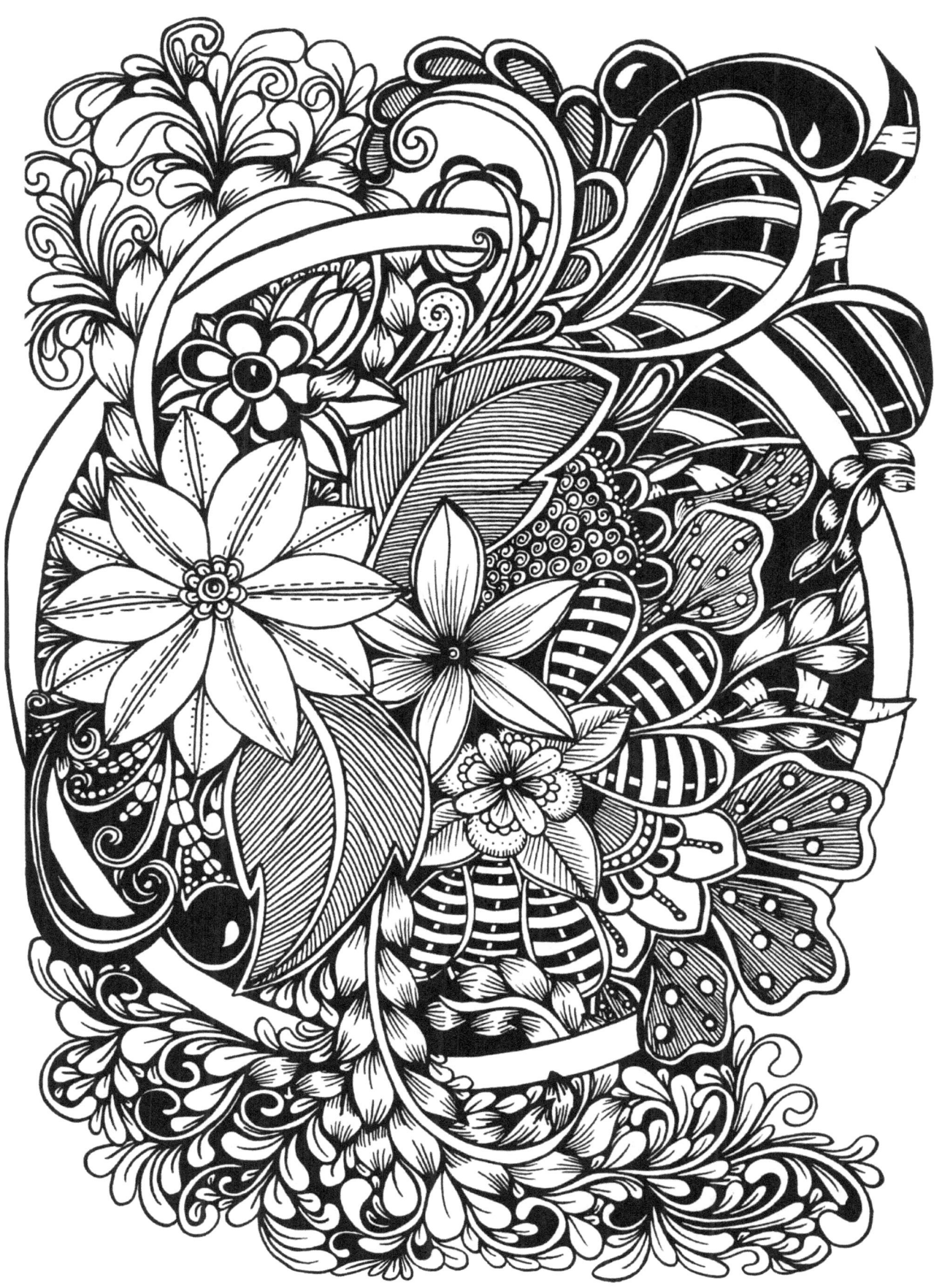

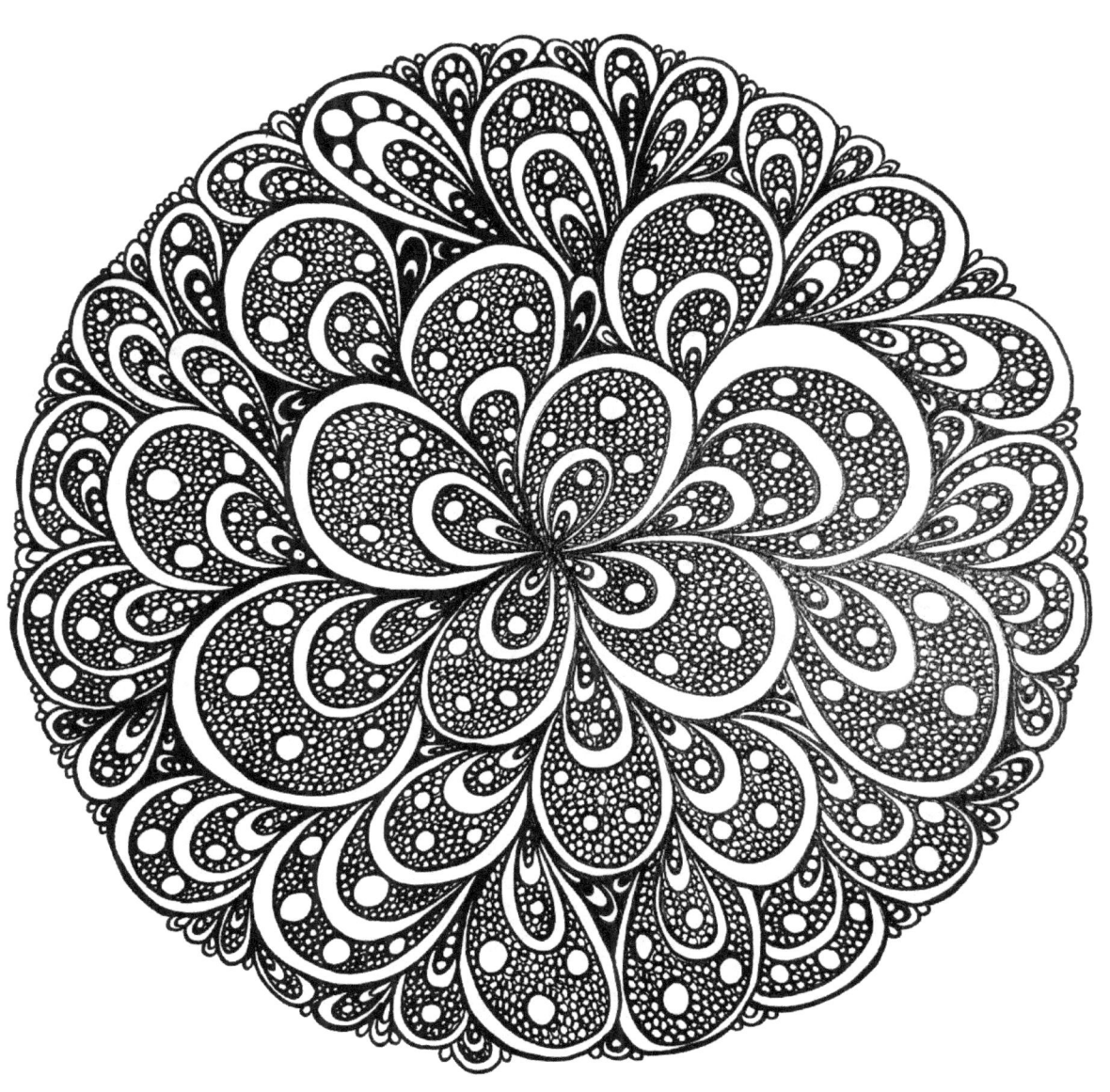

Have you enjoyed this coloring experience?

Your feedback would help me tremendously! Therefore, I ask for you to write me your most honest review on the page of Amazon purchase, as that would be greatly appreciated.

My first coloring book is also available on Amazon, so go ahead and make this collection complete by checking out my 1st edition coloring book.

Stay up-to-date for all my brand new illustration ideas on my Instagram, where I share how these drawings become alive almost daily!

You can find my video's and new post daily, which I share daily on Instagram: @ZentangleArtStory

Anna Zubarev
Illustrator & Coloring Book creator